Che

Tasting journal

This journal belongs to:

_____

Index

Page	Cheese Name	Page	Cheese Name

Index

Page	Cheese Name	Page	Cheese Name

Index

Page	Cheese Name	Page	Cheese Name

Name:

Origin: _____

Producer: _____

Age: _____ Date : _____

Price: _____

Milk

- ☐ Cow
- ☐ Sheep
- ☐ Goat
- ☐ Raw
- ☐ Other
- _____
- _____
- _____

Texture

- ☐ Runny
- ☐ Soft
- ☐ Semi-soft
- ☐ Semi-firm
- ☐ Firm
- ☐ Hard

Notes

_____
_____
_____
_____
_____
_____
_____
_____
_____

Flavors

☐ Buttery ___%	☐ Lingering ___%	☐ Spicy ___%
☐ Grassy ___%	☐ Nutty ___%	☐ Sweet ___%
☐ Earthy ___%	☐ Pungent ___%	☐ Toasty ___%
☐ Herbal ___%	☐ Salty ___%	☐ ___ ___%
☐ Lactic ___%	☐ Sharp ___%	☐ ___ ___%

Rating

Appearance ☆☆☆☆☆ Comments: _____

Aroma ☆☆☆☆☆ _____

Taste ☆☆☆☆☆ _____

Overall Rating ☆☆☆☆☆   Buy Again: ◯ Yes   ◯ No

Name:

Origin: _____

Producer: _____

Age: _____ Date : _____

Price: _____

Milk

- ☐ Cow
- ☐ Sheep
- ☐ Goat
- ☐ Raw
- ☐ Other

_____

_____

_____

Texture

- ☐ Runny
- ☐ Soft
- ☐ Semi-soft
- ☐ Semi-firm
- ☐ Firm
- ☐ Hard

Notes

_____

_____

_____

_____

_____

_____

_____

_____

Flavors

☐ Buttery ___%	☐ Lingering ___%	☐ Spicy ___%
☐ Grassy ___%	☐ Nutty ___%	☐ Sweet ___%
☐ Earthy ___%	☐ Pungent ___%	☐ Toasty ___%
☐ Herbal ___%	☐ Salty ___%	☐ _____ ___%
☐ Lactic ___%	☐ Sharp ___%	☐ _____ ___%

Rating

Appearance ☆☆☆☆☆	Comments: _____
Aroma ☆☆☆☆☆	_____
Taste ☆☆☆☆☆	_____

Overall Rating ☆☆☆☆☆   Buy Again: ○ Yes   ○ No

Name:

Origin:_____

Producer:_____

Age:_____ Date :_____

Price:_____

Milk

- ☐ Cow
- ☐ Sheep
- ☐ Goat
- ☐ Raw
- ☐ Other
- _____
- _____
- _____

Texture

- ☐ Runny
- ☐ Soft
- ☐ Semi-soft
- ☐ Semi-firm
- ☐ Firm
- ☐ Hard

Notes

_____
_____
_____
_____
_____
_____
_____
_____

Flavors

☐ Buttery ___%	☐ Lingering ___%	☐ Spicy ___%
☐ Grassy ___%	☐ Nutty ___%	☐ Sweet ___%
☐ Earthy ___%	☐ Pungent ___%	☐ Toasty ___%
☐ Herbal ___%	☐ Salty ___%	☐ _____ ___%
☐ Lactic ___%	☐ Sharp ___%	☐ _____ ___%

Rating

Appearance	☆☆☆☆☆	Comments:_____
Aroma	☆☆☆☆☆	_____
Taste	☆☆☆☆☆	_____

Overall Rating ☆☆☆☆☆   Buy Again: ○ Yes   ○ No

Name:

Origin: _____

Producer: _____

Age: _____ Date : _____

Price: _____

Milk

- ☐ Cow
- ☐ Sheep
- ☐ Goat
- ☐ Raw
- ☐ Other
- _____
- _____
- _____

Texture

- ☐ Runny
- ☐ Soft
- ☐ Semi-soft
- ☐ Semi-firm
- ☐ Firm
- ☐ Hard

Notes

_____
_____
_____
_____
_____
_____
_____
_____

Flavors

☐ Buttery ___%	☐ Lingering ___%	☐ Spicy ___%
☐ Grassy ___%	☐ Nutty ___%	☐ Sweet ___%
☐ Earthy ___%	☐ Pungent ___%	☐ Toasty ___%
☐ Herbal ___%	☐ Salty ___%	☐ _____ ___%
☐ Lactic ___%	☐ Sharp ___%	☐ _____ ___%

Rating

Appearance	☆☆☆☆☆	Comments: _____
Aroma	☆☆☆☆☆	_____
Taste	☆☆☆☆☆	_____

Overall Rating ☆☆☆☆☆   Buy Again: ◯ Yes   ◯ No

Name:

Origin:_____

Producer:_____

Age:_____ Date :_____

Price:_____

Milk

- ☐ Cow
- ☐ Sheep
- ☐ Goat
- ☐ Raw
- ☐ Other

_____
_____
_____

Texture

- ☐ Runny
- ☐ Soft
- ☐ Semi-soft
- ☐ Semi-firm
- ☐ Firm
- ☐ Hard

Notes

_____
_____
_____
_____
_____
_____
_____
_____

Flavors

☐ Buttery ___%	☐ Lingering ___%	☐ Spicy ___%
☐ Grassy ___%	☐ Nutty ___%	☐ Sweet ___%
☐ Earthy ___%	☐ Pungent ___%	☐ Toasty ___%
☐ Herbal ___%	☐ Salty ___%	☐ _____ ___%
☐ Lactic ___%	☐ Sharp ___%	☐ _____ ___%

Rating

Appearance	☆☆☆☆☆	Comments:_____
Aroma	☆☆☆☆☆	_____
Taste	☆☆☆☆☆	_____

Overall Rating ☆☆☆☆☆   Buy Again: ○ Yes   ○ No

Name:

Origin: _____

Producer: _____

Age: _____ Date : _____

Price: _____

Milk

- ☐ Cow
- ☐ Sheep
- ☐ Goat
- ☐ Raw
- ☐ Other

_____
_____
_____

Texture

- ☐ Runny
- ☐ Soft
- ☐ Semi-soft
- ☐ Semi-firm
- ☐ Firm
- ☐ Hard

Notes

_____
_____
_____
_____
_____
_____
_____
_____

Flavors

☐ Buttery ___%	☐ Lingering ___%	☐ Spicy ___%
☐ Grassy ___%	☐ Nutty ___%	☐ Sweet ___%
☐ Earthy ___%	☐ Pungent ___%	☐ Toasty ___%
☐ Herbal ___%	☐ Salty ___%	☐ ___ ___%
☐ Lactic ___%	☐ Sharp ___%	☐ ___ ___%

Rating

Appearance ☆☆☆☆☆   Comments: _____

Aroma ☆☆☆☆☆   _____

Taste ☆☆☆☆☆   _____

Overall Rating ☆☆☆☆☆   Buy Again: ○ Yes   ○ No

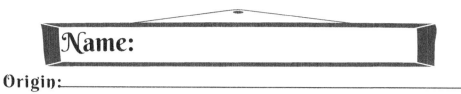

Name:

Origin:

Producer:

Age: _____ Date : _____

Price:

Milk

- ☐ Cow
- ☐ Sheep
- ☐ Goat
- ☐ Raw
- ☐ Other
- _____
- _____
- _____

Texture

- ☐ Runny
- ☐ Soft
- ☐ Semi-soft
- ☐ Semi-firm
- ☐ Firm
- ☐ Hard

Notes

Flavors

☐ Buttery ___%	☐ Lingering ___%	☐ Spicy ___%
☐ Grassy ___%	☐ Nutty ___%	☐ Sweet ___%
☐ Earthy ___%	☐ Pungent ___%	☐ Toasty ___%
☐ Herbal ___%	☐ Salty ___%	☐ _____ ___%
☐ Lactic ___%	☐ Sharp ___%	☐ _____ ___%

Rating

Appearance ☆☆☆☆☆   Comments:

Aroma ☆☆☆☆☆

Taste ☆☆☆☆☆

Overall Rating ☆☆☆☆☆   Buy Again: ○ Yes   ○ No

Name:

Origin:_____

Producer:_____

Age:_____ Date :_____

Price:_____

Milk

- ☐ Cow
- ☐ Sheep
- ☐ Goat
- ☐ Raw
- ☐ Other
- _____
- _____
- _____

Texture

- ☐ Runny
- ☐ Soft
- ☐ Semi-soft
- ☐ Semi-firm
- ☐ Firm
- ☐ Hard

Notes

_____
_____
_____
_____
_____
_____
_____
_____

Flavors

☐ Buttery ___%	☐ Lingering ___%	☐ Spicy ___%
☐ Grassy ___%	☐ Nutty ___%	☐ Sweet ___%
☐ Earthy ___%	☐ Pungent ___%	☐ Toasty ___%
☐ Herbal ___%	☐ Salty ___%	☐ ___ ___%
☐ Lactic ___%	☐ Sharp ___%	☐ ___ ___%

Rating

Appearance	☆☆☆☆☆	Comments:_____
Aroma	☆☆☆☆☆	_____
Taste	☆☆☆☆☆	_____

Overall Rating ☆☆☆☆☆   Buy Again: ◯ Yes   ◯ No

Name:

Origin:_____

Producer:_____

Age:_____ Date : _____

Price:_____

Milk

- ☐ Cow
- ☐ Sheep
- ☐ Goat
- ☐ Raw
- ☐ Other
- _____
- _____
- _____

Texture

- ☐ Runny
- ☐ Soft
- ☐ Semi-soft
- ☐ Semi-firm
- ☐ Firm
- ☐ Hard

Notes

_____
_____
_____
_____
_____
_____
_____
_____
_____

Flavors

☐ Buttery ___%	☐ Lingering ___%	☐ Spicy ___%
☐ Grassy ___%	☐ Nutty ___%	☐ Sweet ___%
☐ Earthy ___%	☐ Pungent ___%	☐ Toasty ___%
☐ Herbal ___%	☐ Salty ___%	☐ _____ ___%
☐ Lactic ___%	☐ Sharp ___%	☐ _____ ___%

Rating

Appearance ☆☆☆☆☆   Comments:_____

Aroma ☆☆☆☆☆   _____

Taste ☆☆☆☆☆   _____

Overall Rating ☆☆☆☆☆   Buy Again: ○ Yes   ○ No

Name:

Origin: _____

Producer: _____

Age: _____ Date : _____

Price: _____

Milk

☐ Cow
☐ Sheep
☐ Goat
☐ Raw
☐ Other
_____
_____
_____

Texture

☐ Runny
☐ Soft
☐ Semi-soft
☐ Semi-firm
☐ Firm
☐ Hard

Notes

_____
_____
_____
_____
_____
_____
_____
_____

Flavors

☐ Buttery __%   ☐ Lingering __%   ☐ Spicy __%
☐ Grassy __%   ☐ Nutty __%   ☐ Sweet __%
☐ Earthy __%   ☐ Pungent __%   ☐ Toasty __%
☐ Herbal __%   ☐ Salty __%   ☐ ____ __%
☐ Lactic __%   ☐ Sharp __%   ☐ ____ __%

Rating

Appearance ☆☆☆☆☆   Comments: _____
Aroma ☆☆☆☆☆   _____
Taste ☆☆☆☆☆   _____

Overall Rating ☆☆☆☆☆   Buy Again: ○ Yes   ○ No

Name:

Origin: _____

Producer: _____

Age: _____ **Date :** _____

Price: _____

Milk

- ☐ Cow
- ☐ Sheep
- ☐ Goat
- ☐ Raw
- ☐ Other
- _____
- _____
- _____

Texture

- ☐ Runny
- ☐ Soft
- ☐ Semi-soft
- ☐ Semi-firm
- ☐ Firm
- ☐ Hard

Notes

_____
_____
_____
_____
_____
_____
_____
_____

Flavors

☐ Buttery ___%	☐ Lingering ___%	☐ Spicy ___%
☐ Grassy ___%	☐ Nutty ___%	☐ Sweet ___%
☐ Earthy ___%	☐ Pungent ___%	☐ Toasty ___%
☐ Herbal ___%	☐ Salty ___%	☐ _____ ___%
☐ Lactic ___%	☐ Sharp ___%	☐ _____ ___%

Rating

Appearance	☆☆☆☆☆	Comments: _____
Aroma	☆☆☆☆☆	_____
Taste	☆☆☆☆☆	_____

Overall Rating ☆☆☆☆☆ **Buy Again:** ◯ Yes   ◯ No

Name:

Origin: _____

Producer: _____

Age: _____ **Date :** _____

Price: _____

Milk

- ☐ Cow
- ☐ Sheep
- ☐ Goat
- ☐ Raw
- ☐ Other
- _____
- _____
- _____

Texture

- ☐ Runny
- ☐ Soft
- ☐ Semi-soft
- ☐ Semi-firm
- ☐ Firm
- ☐ Hard

Notes

_____
_____
_____
_____
_____
_____
_____

Flavors

☐ Buttery ___%	☐ Lingering ___%	☐ Spicy ___%
☐ Grassy ___%	☐ Nutty ___%	☐ Sweet ___%
☐ Earthy ___%	☐ Pungent ___%	☐ Toasty ___%
☐ Herbal ___%	☐ Salty ___%	☐ _____ ___%
☐ Lactic ___%	☐ Sharp ___%	☐ _____ ___%

Rating

Appearance ☆☆☆☆☆	Comments: _____
Aroma ☆☆☆☆☆	_____
Taste ☆☆☆☆☆	_____

Overall Rating ☆☆☆☆☆ **Buy Again:** ○ Yes ○ No

Name:

Origin: _____

Producer: _____

Age: _____ Date : _____

Price: _____

Milk

☐ Cow
☐ Sheep
☐ Goat
☐ Raw
☐ Other
_____
_____
_____

Texture

☐ Runny
☐ Soft
☐ Semi-soft
☐ Semi-firm
☐ Firm
☐ Hard

Notes

_____
_____
_____
_____
_____
_____
_____
_____
_____

Flavors

☐ Buttery ___%   ☐ Lingering ___%   ☐ Spicy ___%
☐ Grassy ___%   ☐ Nutty ___%   ☐ Sweet ___%
☐ Earthy ___%   ☐ Pungent ___%   ☐ Toasty ___%
☐ Herbal ___%   ☐ Salty ___%   ☐ _____ ___%
☐ Lactic ___%   ☐ Sharp ___%   ☐ _____ ___%

Rating

Appearance ☆☆☆☆☆   Comments: _____
Aroma ☆☆☆☆☆   _____
Taste ☆☆☆☆☆   _____

Overall Rating ☆☆☆☆☆   Buy Again: ○ Yes   ○ No

Name:

Origin: _____

Producer: _____

Age: _____ Date : _____

Price: _____

Milk

- ☐ Cow
- ☐ Sheep
- ☐ Goat
- ☐ Raw
- ☐ Other
- _____
- _____
- _____

Texture

- ☐ Runny
- ☐ Soft
- ☐ Semi-soft
- ☐ Semi-firm
- ☐ Firm
- ☐ Hard

Notes

_____
_____
_____
_____
_____
_____
_____
_____

Flavors

☐ Buttery ___%	☐ Lingering ___%	☐ Spicy ___%
☐ Grassy ___%	☐ Nutty ___%	☐ Sweet ___%
☐ Earthy ___%	☐ Pungent ___%	☐ Toasty ___%
☐ Herbal ___%	☐ Salty ___%	☐ _____ ___%
☐ Lactic ___%	☐ Sharp ___%	☐ _____ ___%

Rating

		Comments: _____
Appearance	☆☆☆☆☆	_____
Aroma	☆☆☆☆☆	_____
Taste	☆☆☆☆☆	

Overall Rating ☆☆☆☆☆　　Buy Again: ○ Yes　○ No

Name:

Origin: _____

Producer: _____

Age: _____ Date : _____

Price: _____

Milk

- ☐ Cow
- ☐ Sheep
- ☐ Goat
- ☐ Raw
- ☐ Other

_____
_____
_____

Texture

- ☐ Runny
- ☐ Soft
- ☐ Semi-soft
- ☐ Semi-firm
- ☐ Firm
- ☐ Hard

Notes

_____
_____
_____
_____
_____
_____
_____
_____

Flavors

☐ Buttery ___%	☐ Lingering ___%	☐ Spicy ___%
☐ Grassy ___%	☐ Nutty ___%	☐ Sweet ___%
☐ Earthy ___%	☐ Pungent ___%	☐ Toasty ___%
☐ Herbal ___%	☐ Salty ___%	☐ ___ ___%
☐ Lactic ___%	☐ Sharp ___%	☐ ___ ___%

Rating

Appearance	☆☆☆☆☆	Comments: _____
Aroma	☆☆☆☆☆	_____
Taste	☆☆☆☆☆	_____

Overall Rating ☆☆☆☆☆   Buy Again: ○ Yes   ○ No

Name:

Origin: _____

Producer: _____

Age: _____ Date: _____

Price: _____

Milk

- ☐ Cow
- ☐ Sheep
- ☐ Goat
- ☐ Raw
- ☐ Other
- _____
- _____
- _____

Texture

- ☐ Runny
- ☐ Soft
- ☐ Semi-soft
- ☐ Semi-firm
- ☐ Firm
- ☐ Hard

Notes

_____
_____
_____
_____
_____
_____
_____

Flavors

- ☐ Buttery ___%
- ☐ Grassy ___%
- ☐ Earthy ___%
- ☐ Herbal ___%
- ☐ Lactic ___%
- ☐ Lingering ___%
- ☐ Nutty ___%
- ☐ Pungent ___%
- ☐ Salty ___%
- ☐ Sharp ___%
- ☐ Spicy ___%
- ☐ Sweet ___%
- ☐ Toasty ___%
- ☐ _____ ___%
- ☐ _____ ___%

Rating

Appearance	☆☆☆☆☆	Comments: _____
Aroma	☆☆☆☆☆	_____
Taste	☆☆☆☆☆	_____

Overall Rating ☆☆☆☆☆ Buy Again: ○ Yes ○ No

Name:

Origin:_____

Producer:_____

Age:_____ Date :_____

Price:_____

Milk

- ☐ Cow
- ☐ Sheep
- ☐ Goat
- ☐ Raw
- ☐ Other

_____

_____

_____

Texture

- ☐ Runny
- ☐ Soft
- ☐ Semi-soft
- ☐ Semi-firm
- ☐ Firm
- ☐ Hard

Notes

_____

_____

_____

_____

_____

_____

_____

_____

_____

_____

Flavors

☐ Buttery ___%	☐ Lingering ___%	☐ Spicy ___%
☐ Grassy ___%	☐ Nutty ___%	☐ Sweet ___%
☐ Earthy ___%	☐ Pungent ___%	☐ Toasty ___%
☐ Herbal ___%	☐ Salty ___%	☐ _____ ___%
☐ Lactic ___%	☐ Sharp ___%	☐ _____ ___%

Rating

Appearance	☆☆☆☆☆	Comments:_____
Aroma	☆☆☆☆☆	_____
Taste	☆☆☆☆☆	_____

Overall Rating ☆☆☆☆☆   Buy Again: ○ Yes   ○ No

Name:

Origin: _____

Producer: _____

Age: _____ Date : _____

Price: _____

Milk

- ☐ Cow
- ☐ Sheep
- ☐ Goat
- ☐ Raw
- ☐ Other
- _____
- _____
- _____

Texture

- ☐ Runny
- ☐ Soft
- ☐ Semi-soft
- ☐ Semi-firm
- ☐ Firm
- ☐ Hard

Notes

_____
_____
_____
_____
_____
_____
_____
_____
_____
_____

Flavors

☐ Buttery ___%	☐ Lingering ___%	☐ Spicy ___%
☐ Grassy ___%	☐ Nutty ___%	☐ Sweet ___%
☐ Earthy ___%	☐ Pungent ___%	☐ Toasty ___%
☐ Herbal ___%	☐ Salty ___%	☐ _____ ___%
☐ Lactic ___%	☐ Sharp ___%	☐ _____ ___%

Rating

Appearance ☆☆☆☆☆	Comments: _____
Aroma ☆☆☆☆☆	_____
Taste ☆☆☆☆☆	_____

Overall Rating ☆☆☆☆☆   Buy Again: ○ Yes   ○ No

Name:

Origin: _____

Producer: _____

Age: _____ Date : _____

Price: _____

Milk

- ☐ Cow
- ☐ Sheep
- ☐ Goat
- ☐ Raw
- ☐ Other

_____
_____
_____

Texture

- ☐ Runny
- ☐ Soft
- ☐ Semi-soft
- ☐ Semi-firm
- ☐ Firm
- ☐ Hard

Notes

_____
_____
_____
_____
_____
_____
_____
_____

Flavors

- ☐ Buttery ___%
- ☐ Grassy ___%
- ☐ Earthy ___%
- ☐ Herbal ___%
- ☐ Lactic ___%

- ☐ Lingering ___%
- ☐ Nutty ___%
- ☐ Pungent ___%
- ☐ Salty ___%
- ☐ Sharp ___%

- ☐ Spicy ___%
- ☐ Sweet ___%
- ☐ Toasty ___%
- ☐ _____ ___%
- ☐ _____ ___%

Rating

Appearance	☆☆☆☆☆	Comments: _____
Aroma	☆☆☆☆☆	_____
Taste	☆☆☆☆☆	_____

Overall Rating ☆☆☆☆☆   Buy Again: ○ Yes   ○ No

Name:

Origin: _____

Producer: _____

Age: _____ Date : _____

Price: _____

Milk

☐ Cow
☐ Sheep
☐ Goat
☐ Raw
☐ Other
_____
_____
_____

Texture

☐ Runny
☐ Soft
☐ Semi-soft
☐ Semi-firm
☐ Firm
☐ Hard

Notes

_____
_____
_____
_____
_____
_____
_____
_____
_____

Flavors

☐ Buttery ___%	☐ Lingering ___%	☐ Spicy ___%
☐ Grassy ___%	☐ Nutty ___%	☐ Sweet ___%
☐ Earthy ___%	☐ Pungent ___%	☐ Toasty ___%
☐ Herbal ___%	☐ Salty ___%	☐ _____ ___%
☐ Lactic ___%	☐ Sharp ___%	☐ _____ ___%

Rating

Appearance	☆☆☆☆☆	Comments: _____
Aroma	☆☆☆☆☆	_____
Taste	☆☆☆☆☆	_____

Overall Rating ☆☆☆☆☆   Buy Again: ○ Yes   ○ No

Name:

Origin: _____

Producer: _____

Age: _____ Date : _____

Price: _____

Milk

- ☐ Cow
- ☐ Sheep
- ☐ Goat
- ☐ Raw
- ☐ Other
- _____
- _____
- _____

Texture

- ☐ Runny
- ☐ Soft
- ☐ Semi-soft
- ☐ Semi-firm
- ☐ Firm
- ☐ Hard

Notes

_____
_____
_____
_____
_____
_____
_____
_____
_____
_____

Flavors

☐ Buttery ___%	☐ Lingering ___%	☐ Spicy ___%
☐ Grassy ___%	☐ Nutty ___%	☐ Sweet ___%
☐ Earthy ___%	☐ Pungent ___%	☐ Toasty ___%
☐ Herbal ___%	☐ Salty ___%	☐ _____ ___%
☐ Lactic ___%	☐ Sharp ___%	☐ _____ ___%

Rating

Appearance	☆☆☆☆☆	Comments: _____
Aroma	☆☆☆☆☆	_____
Taste	☆☆☆☆☆	_____

Overall Rating ☆☆☆☆☆   Buy Again: ◯ Yes   ◯ No

Name:

Origin: _____

Producer: _____

Age: _____ Date : _____

Price: _____

Milk

- ☐ Cow
- ☐ Sheep
- ☐ Goat
- ☐ Raw
- ☐ Other

_____

_____

_____

Texture

- ☐ Runny
- ☐ Soft
- ☐ Semi-soft
- ☐ Semi-firm
- ☐ Firm
- ☐ Hard

Notes

_____

_____

_____

_____

_____

_____

_____

_____

_____

Flavors

☐ Buttery ___%	☐ Lingering ___%	☐ Spicy ___%
☐ Grassy ___%	☐ Nutty ___%	☐ Sweet ___%
☐ Earthy ___%	☐ Pungent ___%	☐ Toasty ___%
☐ Herbal ___%	☐ Salty ___%	☐ ___ ___%
☐ Lactic ___%	☐ Sharp ___%	☐ ___ ___%

Rating

Appearance	☆☆☆☆☆	Comments: _____
Aroma	☆☆☆☆☆	_____
Taste	☆☆☆☆☆	_____

Overall Rating ☆☆☆☆☆   Buy Again: ◯ Yes   ◯ No

Name:

Origin: _____

Producer: _____

Age: _____ Date : _____

Price: _____

Milk

- ☐ Cow
- ☐ Sheep
- ☐ Goat
- ☐ Raw
- ☐ Other
- _____
- _____
- _____

Texture

- ☐ Runny
- ☐ Soft
- ☐ Semi-soft
- ☐ Semi-firm
- ☐ Firm
- ☐ Hard

Notes

_____
_____
_____
_____
_____
_____
_____
_____

Flavors

☐ Buttery ___%	☐ Lingering ___%	☐ Spicy ___%
☐ Grassy ___%	☐ Nutty ___%	☐ Sweet ___%
☐ Earthy ___%	☐ Pungent ___%	☐ Toasty ___%
☐ Herbal ___%	☐ Salty ___%	☐ _____ ___%
☐ Lactic ___%	☐ Sharp ___%	☐ _____ ___%

Rating

Appearance	☆☆☆☆☆	Comments: _____
Aroma	☆☆☆☆☆	_____
Taste	☆☆☆☆☆	_____

Overall Rating ☆☆☆☆☆   Buy Again: ◯ Yes   ◯ No

Name:

Origin: _____

Producer: _____

Age: _____ Date: _____

Price: _____

Milk

- ☐ Cow
- ☐ Sheep
- ☐ Goat
- ☐ Raw
- ☐ Other
- _____
- _____
- _____

Texture

- ☐ Runny
- ☐ Soft
- ☐ Semi-soft
- ☐ Semi-firm
- ☐ Firm
- ☐ Hard

Notes

_____
_____
_____
_____
_____
_____
_____
_____
_____

Flavors

☐ Buttery ___%	☐ Lingering ___%	☐ Spicy ___%
☐ Grassy ___%	☐ Nutty ___%	☐ Sweet ___%
☐ Earthy ___%	☐ Pungent ___%	☐ Toasty ___%
☐ Herbal ___%	☐ Salty ___%	☐ _____ ___%
☐ Lactic ___%	☐ Sharp ___%	☐ _____ ___%

Rating

Appearance ☆☆☆☆☆	Comments: _____
Aroma ☆☆☆☆☆	_____
Taste ☆☆☆☆☆	_____

Overall Rating ☆☆☆☆☆   Buy Again: ○ Yes   ○ No

Name:

Origin: _____

Producer: _____

Age: _____ Date : _____

Price: _____

Milk

- ☐ Cow
- ☐ Sheep
- ☐ Goat
- ☐ Raw
- ☐ Other
- _____
- _____
- _____

Texture

- ☐ Runny
- ☐ Soft
- ☐ Semi-soft
- ☐ Semi-firm
- ☐ Firm
- ☐ Hard

Notes

_____
_____
_____
_____
_____
_____
_____
_____

Flavors

- ☐ Buttery ___%
- ☐ Grassy ___%
- ☐ Earthy ___%
- ☐ Herbal ___%
- ☐ Lactic ___%
- ☐ Lingering ___%
- ☐ Nutty ___%
- ☐ Pungent ___%
- ☐ Salty ___%
- ☐ Sharp ___%
- ☐ Spicy ___%
- ☐ Sweet ___%
- ☐ Toasty ___%
- ☐ _____ ___%
- ☐ _____ ___%

Rating

Appearance ☆☆☆☆☆   Comments: _____

Aroma ☆☆☆☆☆   _____

Taste ☆☆☆☆☆   _____

Overall Rating ☆☆☆☆☆   Buy Again: ○ Yes   ○ No

Name:

Origin: _____

Producer: _____

Age: _____ Date : _____

Price: _____

Milk

- ☐ Cow
- ☐ Sheep
- ☐ Goat
- ☐ Raw
- ☐ Other

_____
_____
_____

Texture

- ☐ Runny
- ☐ Soft
- ☐ Semi-soft
- ☐ Semi-firm
- ☐ Firm
- ☐ Hard

Notes

_____
_____
_____
_____
_____
_____
_____
_____

Flavors

☐ Buttery ___%	☐ Lingering ___%	☐ Spicy ___%
☐ Grassy ___%	☐ Nutty ___%	☐ Sweet ___%
☐ Earthy ___%	☐ Pungent ___%	☐ Toasty ___%
☐ Herbal ___%	☐ Salty ___%	☐ _____ ___%
☐ Lactic ___%	☐ Sharp ___%	☐ _____ ___%

Rating

Appearance ☆☆☆☆☆   Comments: _____

Aroma ☆☆☆☆☆   _____

Taste ☆☆☆☆☆   _____

Overall Rating ☆☆☆☆☆   Buy Again: ◯ Yes   ◯ No

Name:

Origin: _____

Producer: _____

Age: _____ Date : _____

Price: _____

Milk

- ☐ Cow
- ☐ Sheep
- ☐ Goat
- ☐ Raw
- ☐ Other

_____
_____
_____

Texture

- ☐ Runny
- ☐ Soft
- ☐ Semi-soft
- ☐ Semi-firm
- ☐ Firm
- ☐ Hard

Notes

_____
_____
_____
_____
_____
_____
_____
_____
_____

Flavors

☐ Buttery ___%	☐ Lingering ___%	☐ Spicy ___%
☐ Grassy ___%	☐ Nutty ___%	☐ Sweet ___%
☐ Earthy ___%	☐ Pungent ___%	☐ Toasty ___%
☐ Herbal ___%	☐ Salty ___%	☐ _____ ___%
☐ Lactic ___%	☐ Sharp ___%	☐ _____ ___%

Rating

Appearance ☆☆☆☆☆	Comments: _____
Aroma ☆☆☆☆☆	_____
Taste ☆☆☆☆☆	_____

Overall Rating ☆☆☆☆☆　　Buy Again: ○ Yes ○ No

Name:

Origin:_____

Producer:_____

Age:_____ Date :_____

Price:_____

Milk
- ☐ Cow
- ☐ Sheep
- ☐ Goat
- ☐ Raw
- ☐ Other
- _____
- _____
- _____

Texture
- ☐ Runny
- ☐ Soft
- ☐ Semi-soft
- ☐ Semi-firm
- ☐ Firm
- ☐ Hard

Notes
_____
_____
_____
_____
_____
_____
_____
_____

Flavors
☐ Buttery ___%	☐ Lingering ___%	☐ Spicy ___%
☐ Grassy ___%	☐ Nutty ___%	☐ Sweet ___%
☐ Earthy ___%	☐ Pungent ___%	☐ Toasty ___%
☐ Herbal ___%	☐ Salty ___%	☐ ____ ___%
☐ Lactic ___%	☐ Sharp ___%	☐ ____ ___%

Rating
Appearance ☆☆☆☆☆   Comments:_____

Aroma ☆☆☆☆☆   _____

Taste ☆☆☆☆☆   _____

Overall Rating ☆☆☆☆☆   Buy Again: ○ Yes   ○ No

Name:

Origin: _____

Producer: _____

Age: _____ Date : _____

Price: _____

Milk

- ☐ Cow
- ☐ Sheep
- ☐ Goat
- ☐ Raw
- ☐ Other

_____
_____
_____

Texture

- ☐ Runny
- ☐ Soft
- ☐ Semi-soft
- ☐ Semi-firm
- ☐ Firm
- ☐ Hard

Notes

_____
_____
_____
_____
_____
_____
_____
_____

Flavors

☐ Buttery ___%	☐ Lingering ___%	☐ Spicy ___%
☐ Grassy ___%	☐ Nutty ___%	☐ Sweet ___%
☐ Earthy ___%	☐ Pungent ___%	☐ Toasty ___%
☐ Herbal ___%	☐ Salty ___%	☐ _____ ___%
☐ Lactic ___%	☐ Sharp ___%	☐ _____ ___%

Rating

Appearance ☆☆☆☆☆   Comments: _____

Aroma ☆☆☆☆☆   _____

Taste ☆☆☆☆☆   _____

Overall Rating ☆☆☆☆☆   Buy Again: ◯ Yes   ◯ No

Name:

Origin: _____

Producer: _____

Age: _____ **Date :** _____

Price: _____

Milk

- ☐ Cow
- ☐ Sheep
- ☐ Goat
- ☐ Raw
- ☐ Other
- _____
- _____
- _____

Texture

- ☐ Runny
- ☐ Soft
- ☐ Semi-soft
- ☐ Semi-firm
- ☐ Firm
- ☐ Hard

Notes

_____
_____
_____
_____
_____
_____
_____
_____

Flavors

- ☐ Buttery ___%
- ☐ Grassy ___%
- ☐ Earthy ___%
- ☐ Herbal ___%
- ☐ Lactic ___%

- ☐ Lingering ___%
- ☐ Nutty ___%
- ☐ Pungent ___%
- ☐ Salty ___%
- ☐ Sharp ___%

- ☐ Spicy ___%
- ☐ Sweet ___%
- ☐ Toasty ___%
- ☐ _____ ___%
- ☐ _____ ___%

Rating

Appearance	☆☆☆☆☆	**Comments:** _____
Aroma	☆☆☆☆☆	_____
Taste	☆☆☆☆☆	_____

Overall Rating ☆☆☆☆☆ **Buy Again:** ◯ Yes ◯ No

Name:

Origin: _____

Producer: _____

Age: _____ Date : _____

Price: _____

Milk

- ☐ Cow
- ☐ Sheep
- ☐ Goat
- ☐ Raw
- ☐ Other
- _____
- _____
- _____

Texture

- ☐ Runny
- ☐ Soft
- ☐ Semi-soft
- ☐ Semi-firm
- ☐ Firm
- ☐ Hard

Notes

_____
_____
_____
_____
_____
_____
_____
_____
_____

Flavors

☐ Buttery ___%	☐ Lingering ___%	☐ Spicy ___%
☐ Grassy ___%	☐ Nutty ___%	☐ Sweet ___%
☐ Earthy ___%	☐ Pungent ___%	☐ Toasty ___%
☐ Herbal ___%	☐ Salty ___%	☐ _____ ___%
☐ Lactic ___%	☐ Sharp ___%	☐ _____ ___%

Rating

Appearance	☆☆☆☆☆	Comments: _____
Aroma	☆☆☆☆☆	_____
Taste	☆☆☆☆☆	_____

Overall Rating ☆☆☆☆☆   Buy Again: ◯ Yes   ◯ No

Name:

Origin: _____

Producer: _____

Age: _____ Date : _____

Price: _____

Milk

- ☐ Cow
- ☐ Sheep
- ☐ Goat
- ☐ Raw
- ☐ Other

_____
_____
_____

Texture

- ☐ Runny
- ☐ Soft
- ☐ Semi-soft
- ☐ Semi-firm
- ☐ Firm
- ☐ Hard

Notes

_____
_____
_____
_____
_____
_____
_____
_____

Flavors

☐ Buttery ___%	☐ Lingering ___%	☐ Spicy ___%
☐ Grassy ___%	☐ Nutty ___%	☐ Sweet ___%
☐ Earthy ___%	☐ Pungent ___%	☐ Toasty ___%
☐ Herbal ___%	☐ Salty ___%	☐ _____ ___%
☐ Lactic ___%	☐ Sharp ___%	☐ _____ ___%

Rating

Appearance ☆☆☆☆☆   Comments: _____

Aroma ☆☆☆☆☆   _____

Taste ☆☆☆☆☆   _____

Overall Rating ☆☆☆☆☆   Buy Again: ○ Yes   ○ No

Name:

Origin: _____

Producer: _____

Age: _____ Date : _____

Price: _____

Milk

- ☐ Cow
- ☐ Sheep
- ☐ Goat
- ☐ Raw
- ☐ Other
- _____
- _____
- _____

Texture

- ☐ Runny
- ☐ Soft
- ☐ Semi-soft
- ☐ Semi-firm
- ☐ Firm
- ☐ Hard

Notes

_____
_____
_____
_____
_____
_____
_____
_____
_____

Flavors

☐ Buttery ___%	☐ Lingering ___%	☐ Spicy ___%
☐ Grassy ___%	☐ Nutty ___%	☐ Sweet ___%
☐ Earthy ___%	☐ Pungent ___%	☐ Toasty ___%
☐ Herbal ___%	☐ Salty ___%	☐ _____ ___%
☐ Lactic ___%	☐ Sharp ___%	☐ _____ ___%

Rating

Appearance	☆☆☆☆☆	Comments: _____
Aroma	☆☆☆☆☆	_____
Taste	☆☆☆☆☆	_____

Overall Rating ☆☆☆☆☆   Buy Again: ◯ Yes   ◯ No

Name:

Origin: _____

Producer: _____

Age: _____ Date : _____

Price: _____

Milk
- ☐ Cow
- ☐ Sheep
- ☐ Goat
- ☐ Raw
- ☐ Other
- _____
- _____
- _____

Texture
- ☐ Runny
- ☐ Soft
- ☐ Semi-soft
- ☐ Semi-firm
- ☐ Firm
- ☐ Hard

Notes
_____
_____
_____
_____
_____
_____
_____
_____

Flavors
- ☐ Buttery ___%
- ☐ Grassy ___%
- ☐ Earthy ___%
- ☐ Herbal ___%
- ☐ Lactic ___%
- ☐ Lingering ___%
- ☐ Nutty ___%
- ☐ Pungent ___%
- ☐ Salty ___%
- ☐ Sharp ___%
- ☐ Spicy ___%
- ☐ Sweet ___%
- ☐ Toasty ___%
- ☐ _____ ___%
- ☐ _____ ___%

Rating

		Comments:
Appearance	☆☆☆☆☆	_____
Aroma	☆☆☆☆☆	_____
Taste	☆☆☆☆☆	_____

Overall Rating ☆☆☆☆☆   Buy Again: ◯ Yes   ◯ No

Name:

Origin:_____

Producer:_____

Age:_____ Date : _____

Price:_____

Milk

- ☐ Cow
- ☐ Sheep
- ☐ Goat
- ☐ Raw
- ☐ Other

_____
_____
_____

Texture

- ☐ Runny
- ☐ Soft
- ☐ Semi-soft
- ☐ Semi-firm
- ☐ Firm
- ☐ Hard

Notes

_____
_____
_____
_____
_____
_____
_____
_____
_____

Flavors

☐ Buttery ___%	☐ Lingering ___%	☐ Spicy ___%
☐ Grassy ___%	☐ Nutty ___%	☐ Sweet ___%
☐ Earthy ___%	☐ Pungent ___%	☐ Toasty ___%
☐ Herbal ___%	☐ Salty ___%	☐ _____ ___%
☐ Lactic ___%	☐ Sharp ___%	☐ _____ ___%

Rating

Appearance	☆☆☆☆☆	Comments:_____
Aroma	☆☆☆☆☆	_____
Taste	☆☆☆☆☆	_____

Overall Rating ☆☆☆☆☆   Buy Again: ○ Yes   ○ No

Name:

Origin:_____

Producer:_____

Age:_____ Date :_____

Price:_____

Milk

- ☐ Cow
- ☐ Sheep
- ☐ Goat
- ☐ Raw
- ☐ Other
- _____
- _____
- _____

Texture

- ☐ Runny
- ☐ Soft
- ☐ Semi-soft
- ☐ Semi-firm
- ☐ Firm
- ☐ Hard

Notes

_____
_____
_____
_____
_____
_____
_____
_____

Flavors

☐ Buttery ___%	☐ Lingering ___%	☐ Spicy ___%
☐ Grassy ___%	☐ Nutty ___%	☐ Sweet ___%
☐ Earthy ___%	☐ Pungent ___%	☐ Toasty ___%
☐ Herbal ___%	☐ Salty ___%	☐ _____ ___%
☐ Lactic ___%	☐ Sharp ___%	☐ _____ ___%

Rating

Appearance ☆☆☆☆☆   Comments:_____

Aroma ☆☆☆☆☆   _____

Taste ☆☆☆☆☆   _____

Overall Rating ☆☆☆☆☆   Buy Again: ○ Yes   ○ No

Name:

Origin: _____

Producer: _____

Age: _____ **Date :** _____

Price: _____

Milk

- ☐ Cow
- ☐ Sheep
- ☐ Goat
- ☐ Raw
- ☐ Other
- _____
- _____
- _____

Texture

- ☐ Runny
- ☐ Soft
- ☐ Semi-soft
- ☐ Semi-firm
- ☐ Firm
- ☐ Hard

Notes

_____
_____
_____
_____
_____
_____
_____
_____
_____

Flavors

- ☐ Buttery ___%
- ☐ Grassy ___%
- ☐ Earthy ___%
- ☐ Herbal ___%
- ☐ Lactic ___%
- ☐ Lingering ___%
- ☐ Nutty ___%
- ☐ Pungent ___%
- ☐ Salty ___%
- ☐ Sharp ___%
- ☐ Spicy ___%
- ☐ Sweet ___%
- ☐ Toasty ___%
- ☐ _____ ___%
- ☐ _____ ___%

Rating

Appearance	☆☆☆☆☆	Comments: _____
Aroma	☆☆☆☆☆	_____
Taste	☆☆☆☆☆	_____

Overall Rating ☆☆☆☆☆   **Buy Again:** ◯ Yes   ◯ No

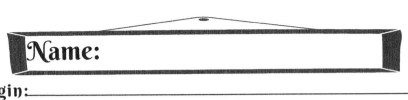

Name:

Origin: _____

Producer: _____

Age: _____ Date : _____

Price: _____

Milk
- ☐ Cow
- ☐ Sheep
- ☐ Goat
- ☐ Raw
- ☐ Other
- _____
- _____
- _____

Texture
- ☐ Runny
- ☐ Soft
- ☐ Semi-soft
- ☐ Semi-firm
- ☐ Firm
- ☐ Hard

Notes
_____
_____
_____
_____
_____
_____
_____
_____
_____

Flavors
☐ Buttery ___%	☐ Lingering ___%	☐ Spicy ___%
☐ Grassy ___%	☐ Nutty ___%	☐ Sweet ___%
☐ Earthy ___%	☐ Pungent ___%	☐ Toasty ___%
☐ Herbal ___%	☐ Salty ___%	☐ _____ ___%
☐ Lactic ___%	☐ Sharp ___%	☐ _____ ___%

Rating
Appearance ☆☆☆☆☆   Comments: _____

Aroma ☆☆☆☆☆   _____

Taste ☆☆☆☆☆   _____

Overall Rating ☆☆☆☆☆   Buy Again: ○ Yes   ○ No

Name:

Origin: _____

Producer: _____

Age: _____ Date : _____

Price: _____

Milk

- ☐ Cow
- ☐ Sheep
- ☐ Goat
- ☐ Raw
- ☐ Other
- _____
- _____
- _____

Texture

- ☐ Runny
- ☐ Soft
- ☐ Semi-soft
- ☐ Semi-firm
- ☐ Firm
- ☐ Hard

Notes

_____
_____
_____
_____
_____
_____
_____
_____
_____
_____

Flavors

☐ Buttery ___%	☐ Lingering ___%	☐ Spicy ___%
☐ Grassy ___%	☐ Nutty ___%	☐ Sweet ___%
☐ Earthy ___%	☐ Pungent ___%	☐ Toasty ___%
☐ Herbal ___%	☐ Salty ___%	☐ _____ ___%
☐ Lactic ___%	☐ Sharp ___%	☐ _____ ___%

Rating

Appearance	☆☆☆☆☆	Comments: _____
Aroma	☆☆☆☆☆	_____
Taste	☆☆☆☆☆	_____

Overall Rating ☆☆☆☆☆   Buy Again: ○ Yes   ○ No

Name:

Origin: _____

Producer: _____

Age: _____ Date : _____

Price: _____

Milk

- ☐ Cow
- ☐ Sheep
- ☐ Goat
- ☐ Raw
- ☐ Other
- _____
- _____
- _____

Texture

- ☐ Runny
- ☐ Soft
- ☐ Semi-soft
- ☐ Semi-firm
- ☐ Firm
- ☐ Hard

Notes

_____
_____
_____
_____
_____
_____
_____
_____
_____

Flavors

☐ Buttery ___%	☐ Lingering ___%	☐ Spicy ___%
☐ Grassy ___%	☐ Nutty ___%	☐ Sweet ___%
☐ Earthy ___%	☐ Pungent ___%	☐ Toasty ___%
☐ Herbal ___%	☐ Salty ___%	☐ _____ ___%
☐ Lactic ___%	☐ Sharp ___%	☐ _____ ___%

Rating

Appearance	☆☆☆☆☆	Comments: _____
Aroma	☆☆☆☆☆	_____
Taste	☆☆☆☆☆	_____

Overall Rating ☆☆☆☆☆   Buy Again: ○ Yes   ○ No

Name:

Origin: _____

Producer: _____

Age: _____ Date : _____

Price: _____

Milk

- ☐ Cow
- ☐ Sheep
- ☐ Goat
- ☐ Raw
- ☐ Other
- _____
- _____
- _____

Texture

- ☐ Runny
- ☐ Soft
- ☐ Semi-soft
- ☐ Semi-firm
- ☐ Firm
- ☐ Hard

Notes

_____
_____
_____
_____
_____
_____
_____
_____
_____

Flavors

☐ Buttery __%	☐ Lingering __%	☐ Spicy __%
☐ Grassy __%	☐ Nutty __%	☐ Sweet __%
☐ Earthy __%	☐ Pungent __%	☐ Toasty __%
☐ Herbal __%	☐ Salty __%	☐ _____ __%
☐ Lactic __%	☐ Sharp __%	☐ _____ __%

Rating

Appearance ☆☆☆☆☆ Comments: _____
Aroma ☆☆☆☆☆ _____
Taste ☆☆☆☆☆ _____

Overall Rating ☆☆☆☆☆ Buy Again: ○ Yes   ○ No

Name:

Origin: _____

Producer: _____

Age: _____ **Date :** _____

Price: _____

Milk

- ☐ Cow
- ☐ Sheep
- ☐ Goat
- ☐ Raw
- ☐ Other

_____
_____
_____

Texture

- ☐ Runny
- ☐ Soft
- ☐ Semi-soft
- ☐ Semi-firm
- ☐ Firm
- ☐ Hard

Notes

_____
_____
_____
_____
_____
_____
_____
_____

Flavors

☐ Buttery ___%	☐ Lingering ___%	☐ Spicy ___%
☐ Grassy ___%	☐ Nutty ___%	☐ Sweet ___%
☐ Earthy ___%	☐ Pungent ___%	☐ Toasty ___%
☐ Herbal ___%	☐ Salty ___%	☐ ___ ___%
☐ Lactic ___%	☐ Sharp ___%	☐ ___ ___%

Rating

Appearance	☆☆☆☆☆	Comments: _____
Aroma	☆☆☆☆☆	_____
Taste	☆☆☆☆☆	_____

Overall Rating ☆☆☆☆☆ **Buy Again:** ○ Yes ○ No

Name:

Origin: _____

Producer: _____

Age: _____ Date : _____

Price: _____

Milk

- ☐ Cow
- ☐ Sheep
- ☐ Goat
- ☐ Raw
- ☐ Other
- _____
- _____
- _____

Texture

- ☐ Runny
- ☐ Soft
- ☐ Semi-soft
- ☐ Semi-firm
- ☐ Firm
- ☐ Hard

Notes

_____
_____
_____
_____
_____
_____
_____
_____

Flavors

- ☐ Buttery ___%
- ☐ Grassy ___%
- ☐ Earthy ___%
- ☐ Herbal ___%
- ☐ Lactic ___%
- ☐ Lingering ___%
- ☐ Nutty ___%
- ☐ Pungent ___%
- ☐ Salty ___%
- ☐ Sharp ___%
- ☐ Spicy ___%
- ☐ Sweet ___%
- ☐ Toasty ___%
- ☐ _____ ___%
- ☐ _____ ___%

Rating

Appearance	☆☆☆☆☆	Comments: _____
Aroma	☆☆☆☆☆	_____
Taste	☆☆☆☆☆	_____

Overall Rating ☆☆☆☆☆   Buy Again: ◯ Yes   ◯ No

Name:

Origin: _____

Producer: _____

Age: _____ Date : _____

Price: _____

Milk

- ☐ Cow
- ☐ Sheep
- ☐ Goat
- ☐ Raw
- ☐ Other

_____
_____
_____

Texture

- ☐ Runny
- ☐ Soft
- ☐ Semi-soft
- ☐ Semi-firm
- ☐ Firm
- ☐ Hard

Notes

_____
_____
_____
_____
_____
_____
_____
_____
_____

Flavors

☐ Buttery ___%	☐ Lingering ___%	☐ Spicy ___%
☐ Grassy ___%	☐ Nutty ___%	☐ Sweet ___%
☐ Earthy ___%	☐ Pungent ___%	☐ Toasty ___%
☐ Herbal ___%	☐ Salty ___%	☐ _____ ___%
☐ Lactic ___%	☐ Sharp ___%	☐ _____ ___%

Rating

Appearance ☆☆☆☆☆   Comments: _____

Aroma ☆☆☆☆☆   _____

Taste ☆☆☆☆☆   _____

Overall Rating ☆☆☆☆☆   Buy Again: ○ Yes   ○ No

Name:

Origin: _____

Producer: _____

Age: _____ Date : _____

Price: _____

Milk

- ☐ Cow
- ☐ Sheep
- ☐ Goat
- ☐ Raw
- ☐ Other

_____

_____

_____

Texture

- ☐ Runny
- ☐ Soft
- ☐ Semi-soft
- ☐ Semi-firm
- ☐ Firm
- ☐ Hard

Notes

_____

_____

_____

_____

_____

_____

_____

_____

Flavors

☐ Buttery ___%	☐ Lingering ___%	☐ Spicy ___%
☐ Grassy ___%	☐ Nutty ___%	☐ Sweet ___%
☐ Earthy ___%	☐ Pungent ___%	☐ Toasty ___%
☐ Herbal ___%	☐ Salty ___%	☐ _____ ___%
☐ Lactic ___%	☐ Sharp ___%	☐ _____ ___%

Rating

Appearance	☆☆☆☆☆	Comments: _____
Aroma	☆☆☆☆☆	_____
Taste	☆☆☆☆☆	_____

Overall Rating ☆☆☆☆☆   Buy Again: ◯ Yes   ◯ No

Name:

Origin: _____

Producer: _____

Age: _____ **Date :** _____

Price: _____

Milk

- ☐ Cow
- ☐ Sheep
- ☐ Goat
- ☐ Raw
- ☐ Other

_____
_____
_____

Texture

- ☐ Runny
- ☐ Soft
- ☐ Semi-soft
- ☐ Semi-firm
- ☐ Firm
- ☐ Hard

Notes

_____
_____
_____
_____
_____
_____
_____
_____

Flavors

☐ Buttery ___%	☐ Lingering ___%	☐ Spicy ___%
☐ Grassy ___%	☐ Nutty ___%	☐ Sweet ___%
☐ Earthy ___%	☐ Pungent ___%	☐ Toasty ___%
☐ Herbal ___%	☐ Salty ___%	☐ _____ ___%
☐ Lactic ___%	☐ Sharp ___%	☐ _____ ___%

Rating

Appearance	☆☆☆☆☆	Comments: _____
Aroma	☆☆☆☆☆	_____
Taste	☆☆☆☆☆	_____

Overall Rating ☆☆☆☆☆   **Buy Again:** ○ Yes   ○ No

Name:

Origin: _____

Producer: _____

Age: _____ **Date :** _____

Price: _____

Milk

- ☐ Cow
- ☐ Sheep
- ☐ Goat
- ☐ Raw
- ☐ Other
- _____
- _____
- _____

Texture

- ☐ Runny
- ☐ Soft
- ☐ Semi-soft
- ☐ Semi-firm
- ☐ Firm
- ☐ Hard

Notes

_____
_____
_____
_____
_____
_____
_____
_____
_____

Flavors

☐ Buttery ___%	☐ Lingering ___%	☐ Spicy ___%
☐ Grassy ___%	☐ Nutty ___%	☐ Sweet ___%
☐ Earthy ___%	☐ Pungent ___%	☐ Toasty ___%
☐ Herbal ___%	☐ Salty ___%	☐ _____ ___%
☐ Lactic ___%	☐ Sharp ___%	☐ _____ ___%

Rating

Appearance	☆☆☆☆☆	Comments: _____
Aroma	☆☆☆☆☆	_____
Taste	☆☆☆☆☆	_____

Overall Rating ☆☆☆☆☆   **Buy Again:** ○ Yes   ○ No

Name:

Origin: _____

Producer: _____

Age: _____ Date : _____

Price: _____

Milk

- ☐ Cow
- ☐ Sheep
- ☐ Goat
- ☐ Raw
- ☐ Other
- _____
- _____
- _____

Texture

- ☐ Runny
- ☐ Soft
- ☐ Semi-soft
- ☐ Semi-firm
- ☐ Firm
- ☐ Hard

Notes

_____
_____
_____
_____
_____
_____
_____
_____

Flavors

☐ Buttery ___%	☐ Lingering ___%	☐ Spicy ___%
☐ Grassy ___%	☐ Nutty ___%	☐ Sweet ___%
☐ Earthy ___%	☐ Pungent ___%	☐ Toasty ___%
☐ Herbal ___%	☐ Salty ___%	☐ _____ ___%
☐ Lactic ___%	☐ Sharp ___%	☐ _____ ___%

Rating

Appearance	☆☆☆☆☆	Comments: _____
Aroma	☆☆☆☆☆	_____
Taste	☆☆☆☆☆	_____

Overall Rating ☆☆☆☆☆   Buy Again: ○ Yes   ○ No

Name:

Origin: _____

Producer: _____

Age: _____ Date : _____

Price: _____

Milk

- ☐ Cow
- ☐ Sheep
- ☐ Goat
- ☐ Raw
- ☐ Other
- _____
- _____
- _____

Texture

- ☐ Runny
- ☐ Soft
- ☐ Semi-soft
- ☐ Semi-firm
- ☐ Firm
- ☐ Hard

Notes

_____
_____
_____
_____
_____
_____
_____
_____
_____
_____

Flavors

- ☐ Buttery ___%
- ☐ Grassy ___%
- ☐ Earthy ___%
- ☐ Herbal ___%
- ☐ Lactic ___%

- ☐ Lingering ___%
- ☐ Nutty ___%
- ☐ Pungent ___%
- ☐ Salty ___%
- ☐ Sharp ___%

- ☐ Spicy ___%
- ☐ Sweet ___%
- ☐ Toasty ___%
- ☐ _____ ___%
- ☐ _____ ___%

Rating

Appearance ☆☆☆☆☆
Aroma ☆☆☆☆☆
Taste ☆☆☆☆☆

Comments: _____
_____
_____

Overall Rating ☆☆☆☆☆   Buy Again: ○ Yes   ○ No

Name:

Origin: _____

Producer: _____

Age: _____ Date : _____

Price: _____

Milk

- ☐ Cow
- ☐ Sheep
- ☐ Goat
- ☐ Raw
- ☐ Other

_____
_____
_____

Texture

- ☐ Runny
- ☐ Soft
- ☐ Semi-soft
- ☐ Semi-firm
- ☐ Firm
- ☐ Hard

Notes

_____
_____
_____
_____
_____
_____
_____
_____

Flavors

☐ Buttery ___%	☐ Lingering ___%	☐ Spicy ___%
☐ Grassy ___%	☐ Nutty ___%	☐ Sweet ___%
☐ Earthy ___%	☐ Pungent ___%	☐ Toasty ___%
☐ Herbal ___%	☐ Salty ___%	☐ _____ ___%
☐ Lactic ___%	☐ Sharp ___%	☐ _____ ___%

Rating

Appearance ☆☆☆☆☆	Comments: _____
Aroma ☆☆☆☆☆	_____
Taste ☆☆☆☆☆	_____

Overall Rating ☆☆☆☆☆   Buy Again: ○ Yes   ○ No

Name:

Origin:_____

Producer:_____

Age:_____ Date : _____

Price:_____

Milk

- ☐ Cow
- ☐ Sheep
- ☐ Goat
- ☐ Raw
- ☐ Other
_____
_____
_____

Texture

- ☐ Runny
- ☐ Soft
- ☐ Semi-soft
- ☐ Semi-firm
- ☐ Firm
- ☐ Hard

Notes

_____
_____
_____
_____
_____
_____
_____
_____
_____

Flavors

☐ Buttery ___%	☐ Lingering ___%	☐ Spicy ___%
☐ Grassy ___%	☐ Nutty ___%	☐ Sweet ___%
☐ Earthy ___%	☐ Pungent ___%	☐ Toasty ___%
☐ Herbal ___%	☐ Salty ___%	☐ ___ ___%
☐ Lactic ___%	☐ Sharp ___%	☐ ___ ___%

Rating

Appearance ☆☆☆☆☆   Comments:_____

Aroma ☆☆☆☆☆   _____

Taste ☆☆☆☆☆   _____

Overall Rating ☆☆☆☆☆   Buy Again: ○ Yes   ○ No

Name:

Origin: _____

Producer: _____

Age: _____ Date : _____

Price: _____

Milk

- ☐ Cow
- ☐ Sheep
- ☐ Goat
- ☐ Raw
- ☐ Other

_____
_____
_____

Texture

- ☐ Runny
- ☐ Soft
- ☐ Semi-soft
- ☐ Semi-firm
- ☐ Firm
- ☐ Hard

Notes

_____
_____
_____
_____
_____
_____
_____
_____
_____
_____

Flavors

☐ Buttery ___%	☐ Lingering ___%	☐ Spicy ___%
☐ Grassy ___%	☐ Nutty ___%	☐ Sweet ___%
☐ Earthy ___%	☐ Pungent ___%	☐ Toasty ___%
☐ Herbal ___%	☐ Salty ___%	☐ _____ ___%
☐ Lactic ___%	☐ Sharp ___%	☐ _____ ___%

Rating

Appearance	☆☆☆☆☆	Comments: _____
Aroma	☆☆☆☆☆	_____
Taste	☆☆☆☆☆	_____

Overall Rating ☆☆☆☆☆   Buy Again: ◯ Yes   ◯ No

Name:

Origin: _____

Producer: _____

Age: _____ Date : _____

Price: _____

Milk

- ☐ Cow
- ☐ Sheep
- ☐ Goat
- ☐ Raw
- ☐ Other
- _____
- _____
- _____

Texture

- ☐ Runny
- ☐ Soft
- ☐ Semi-soft
- ☐ Semi-firm
- ☐ Firm
- ☐ Hard

Notes

_____
_____
_____
_____
_____
_____
_____
_____

Flavors

☐ Buttery ___%	☐ Lingering ___%	☐ Spicy ___%
☐ Grassy ___%	☐ Nutty ___%	☐ Sweet ___%
☐ Earthy ___%	☐ Pungent ___%	☐ Toasty ___%
☐ Herbal ___%	☐ Salty ___%	☐ _____ ___%
☐ Lactic ___%	☐ Sharp ___%	☐ _____ ___%

Rating

Appearance	☆☆☆☆☆	Comments: _____
Aroma	☆☆☆☆☆	_____
Taste	☆☆☆☆☆	_____

Overall Rating ☆☆☆☆☆   Buy Again: ○ Yes   ○ No

Name:

Origin: _____

Producer: _____

Age: _____ Date : _____

Price: _____

Milk
- ☐ Cow
- ☐ Sheep
- ☐ Goat
- ☐ Raw
- ☐ Other
- _____
- _____
- _____

Texture
- ☐ Runny
- ☐ Soft
- ☐ Semi-soft
- ☐ Semi-firm
- ☐ Firm
- ☐ Hard

Notes
_____
_____
_____
_____
_____
_____
_____
_____

Flavors

☐ Buttery ___%	☐ Lingering ___%	☐ Spicy ___%
☐ Grassy ___%	☐ Nutty ___%	☐ Sweet ___%
☐ Earthy ___%	☐ Pungent ___%	☐ Toasty ___%
☐ Herbal ___%	☐ Salty ___%	☐ ____ ___%
☐ Lactic ___%	☐ Sharp ___%	☐ ____ ___%

Rating

Appearance	☆☆☆☆☆	Comments: _____
Aroma	☆☆☆☆☆	_____
Taste	☆☆☆☆☆	_____

Overall Rating ☆☆☆☆☆   Buy Again: ◯ Yes   ◯ No

Name:

Origin: _____

Producer: _____

Age: _____ Date : _____

Price: _____

Milk

☐ Cow
☐ Sheep
☐ Goat
☐ Raw
☐ Other
_____
_____
_____

Texture

☐ Runny
☐ Soft
☐ Semi-soft
☐ Semi-firm
☐ Firm
☐ Hard

Notes

_____
_____
_____
_____
_____
_____
_____
_____
_____

Flavors

☐ Buttery ___%	☐ Lingering ___%	☐ Spicy ___%
☐ Grassy ___%	☐ Nutty ___%	☐ Sweet ___%
☐ Earthy ___%	☐ Pungent ___%	☐ Toasty ___%
☐ Herbal ___%	☐ Salty ___%	☐ _____ ___%
☐ Lactic ___%	☐ Sharp ___%	☐ _____ ___%

Rating

Appearance ☆☆☆☆☆
Aroma ☆☆☆☆☆
Taste ☆☆☆☆☆

Comments: _____
_____
_____

Overall Rating ☆☆☆☆☆   Buy Again: ○ Yes   ○ No

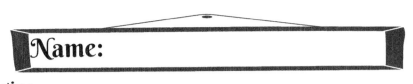

Name:

Origin:_____

Producer:_____

Age:_____ Date :_____

Price:_____

Milk

- ☐ Cow
- ☐ Sheep
- ☐ Goat
- ☐ Raw
- ☐ Other
- _____
- _____
- _____

Texture

- ☐ Runny
- ☐ Soft
- ☐ Semi-soft
- ☐ Semi-firm
- ☐ Firm
- ☐ Hard

Notes

_____
_____
_____
_____
_____
_____
_____
_____

Flavors

☐ Buttery ___%	☐ Lingering ___%	☐ Spicy ___%
☐ Grassy ___%	☐ Nutty ___%	☐ Sweet ___%
☐ Earthy ___%	☐ Pungent ___%	☐ Toasty ___%
☐ Herbal ___%	☐ Salty ___%	☐ ____ ___%
☐ Lactic ___%	☐ Sharp ___%	☐ ____ ___%

Rating

Appearance ☆☆☆☆☆   Comments:_____

Aroma ☆☆☆☆☆   _____

Taste ☆☆☆☆☆   _____

Overall Rating ☆☆☆☆☆   Buy Again: ○ Yes   ○ No

Name:

Origin: _____

Producer: _____

Age: _____ Date : _____

Price: _____

Milk

- ☐ Cow
- ☐ Sheep
- ☐ Goat
- ☐ Raw
- ☐ Other
- _____
- _____
- _____

Texture

- ☐ Runny
- ☐ Soft
- ☐ Semi-soft
- ☐ Semi-firm
- ☐ Firm
- ☐ Hard

Notes

_____
_____
_____
_____
_____
_____
_____
_____
_____

Flavors

☐ Buttery ___%	☐ Lingering ___%	☐ Spicy ___%
☐ Grassy ___%	☐ Nutty ___%	☐ Sweet ___%
☐ Earthy ___%	☐ Pungent ___%	☐ Toasty ___%
☐ Herbal ___%	☐ Salty ___%	☐ _____ ___%
☐ Lactic ___%	☐ Sharp ___%	☐ _____ ___%

Rating

Appearance	☆☆☆☆☆	Comments: _____
Aroma	☆☆☆☆☆	_____
Taste	☆☆☆☆☆	_____

Overall Rating ☆☆☆☆☆   Buy Again: ◯ Yes   ◯ No

Name:

Origin: _____

Producer: _____

Age: _____ Date : _____

Price: _____

Milk

- ☐ Cow
- ☐ Sheep
- ☐ Goat
- ☐ Raw
- ☐ Other
- _____
- _____
- _____

Texture

- ☐ Runny
- ☐ Soft
- ☐ Semi-soft
- ☐ Semi-firm
- ☐ Firm
- ☐ Hard

Notes

_____
_____
_____
_____
_____
_____
_____
_____
_____

Flavors

☐ Buttery __%	☐ Lingering __%	☐ Spicy __%
☐ Grassy __%	☐ Nutty __%	☐ Sweet __%
☐ Earthy __%	☐ Pungent __%	☐ Toasty __%
☐ Herbal __%	☐ Salty __%	☐ _____ __%
☐ Lactic __%	☐ Sharp __%	☐ _____ __%

Rating

Appearance	☆☆☆☆☆	Comments: _____
Aroma	☆☆☆☆☆	_____
Taste	☆☆☆☆☆	_____

Overall Rating ☆☆☆☆☆   Buy Again: ○ Yes   ○ No

Name:

Origin: _____

Producer: _____

Age: _____ **Date :** _____

Price: _____

Milk

- ☐ Cow
- ☐ Sheep
- ☐ Goat
- ☐ Raw
- ☐ Other
- _____
- _____
- _____

Texture

- ☐ Runny
- ☐ Soft
- ☐ Semi-soft
- ☐ Semi-firm
- ☐ Firm
- ☐ Hard

Notes

_____

_____

_____

_____

_____

_____

_____

_____

Flavors

- ☐ Buttery ___%
- ☐ Grassy ___%
- ☐ Earthy ___%
- ☐ Herbal ___%
- ☐ Lactic ___%

- ☐ Lingering ___%
- ☐ Nutty ___%
- ☐ Pungent ___%
- ☐ Salty ___%
- ☐ Sharp ___%

- ☐ Spicy ___%
- ☐ Sweet ___%
- ☐ Toasty ___%
- ☐ _____ ___%
- ☐ _____ ___%

Rating

Appearance	☆☆☆☆☆	Comments: _____
Aroma	☆☆☆☆☆	_____
Taste	☆☆☆☆☆	_____

Overall Rating ☆☆☆☆☆   **Buy Again:** ○ Yes   ○ No

Name:

Origin:_____

Producer:_____

Age:_____ Date : _____

Price: _____

Milk

- ☐ Cow
- ☐ Sheep
- ☐ Goat
- ☐ Raw
- ☐ Other
- _____
- _____
- _____

Texture

- ☐ Runny
- ☐ Soft
- ☐ Semi-soft
- ☐ Semi-firm
- ☐ Firm
- ☐ Hard

Notes

_____
_____
_____
_____
_____
_____
_____
_____

Flavors

☐ Buttery ___%	☐ Lingering ___%	☐ Spicy ___%
☐ Grassy ___%	☐ Nutty ___%	☐ Sweet ___%
☐ Earthy ___%	☐ Pungent ___%	☐ Toasty ___%
☐ Herbal ___%	☐ Salty ___%	☐ ___ ___%
☐ Lactic ___%	☐ Sharp ___%	☐ ___ ___%

Rating

Appearance	☆☆☆☆☆	Comments:_____
Aroma	☆☆☆☆☆	_____
Taste	☆☆☆☆☆	_____

Overall Rating ☆☆☆☆☆   Buy Again: ○ Yes   ○ No

Name:

Origin: _____

Producer: _____

Age: _____ Date : _____

Price: _____

Milk

- ☐ Cow
- ☐ Sheep
- ☐ Goat
- ☐ Raw
- ☐ Other
- _____
- _____
- _____

Texture

- ☐ Runny
- ☐ Soft
- ☐ Semi-soft
- ☐ Semi-firm
- ☐ Firm
- ☐ Hard

Notes

_____
_____
_____
_____
_____
_____
_____
_____

Flavors

☐ Buttery ___%	☐ Lingering ___%	☐ Spicy ___%
☐ Grassy ___%	☐ Nutty ___%	☐ Sweet ___%
☐ Earthy ___%	☐ Pungent ___%	☐ Toasty ___%
☐ Herbal ___%	☐ Salty ___%	☐ ___ ___%
☐ Lactic ___%	☐ Sharp ___%	☐ ___ ___%

Rating

Appearance ☆☆☆☆☆ Comments: _____

Aroma ☆☆☆☆☆ _____

Taste ☆☆☆☆☆ _____

Overall Rating ☆☆☆☆☆   Buy Again: ○ Yes   ○ No

Name:

Origin:_____

Producer:_____

Age:_____ Date : _____

Price:_____

Milk
- ☐ Cow
- ☐ Sheep
- ☐ Goat
- ☐ Raw
- ☐ Other
- _____
- _____
- _____

Texture
- ☐ Runny
- ☐ Soft
- ☐ Semi-soft
- ☐ Semi-firm
- ☐ Firm
- ☐ Hard

Notes
_____
_____
_____
_____
_____
_____
_____
_____

Flavors

☐ Buttery ___%	☐ Lingering ___%	☐ Spicy ___%
☐ Grassy ___%	☐ Nutty ___%	☐ Sweet ___%
☐ Earthy ___%	☐ Pungent ___%	☐ Toasty ___%
☐ Herbal ___%	☐ Salty ___%	☐ _____ ___%
☐ Lactic ___%	☐ Sharp ___%	☐ _____ ___%

Rating

		Comments:
Appearance	☆☆☆☆☆	_____
Aroma	☆☆☆☆☆	_____
Taste	☆☆☆☆☆	_____

Overall Rating ☆☆☆☆☆   Buy Again: ○ Yes   ○ No

Name:

Origin: _____

Producer: _____

Age: _____ Date : _____

Price: _____

Milk

- ☐ Cow
- ☐ Sheep
- ☐ Goat
- ☐ Raw
- ☐ Other

_____
_____
_____

Texture

- ☐ Runny
- ☐ Soft
- ☐ Semi-soft
- ☐ Semi-firm
- ☐ Firm
- ☐ Hard

Notes

_____
_____
_____
_____
_____
_____
_____
_____
_____

Flavors

☐ Buttery ___%	☐ Lingering ___%	☐ Spicy ___%
☐ Grassy ___%	☐ Nutty ___%	☐ Sweet ___%
☐ Earthy ___%	☐ Pungent ___%	☐ Toasty ___%
☐ Herbal ___%	☐ Salty ___%	☐ ___ ___%
☐ Lactic ___%	☐ Sharp ___%	☐ ___ ___%

Rating

Appearance ☆☆☆☆☆   Comments: _____
Aroma ☆☆☆☆☆   _____
Taste ☆☆☆☆☆   _____

Overall Rating ☆☆☆☆☆   Buy Again: ○ Yes   ○ No

Name:

Origin: _____

Producer: _____

Age: _____ Date : _____

Price: _____

Milk

☐ Cow
☐ Sheep
☐ Goat
☐ Raw
☐ Other
_____
_____
_____

Texture

☐ Runny
☐ Soft
☐ Semi-soft
☐ Semi-firm
☐ Firm
☐ Hard

Notes

_____
_____
_____
_____
_____
_____
_____
_____

Flavors

☐ Buttery ___%	☐ Lingering ___%	☐ Spicy ___%
☐ Grassy ___%	☐ Nutty ___%	☐ Sweet ___%
☐ Earthy ___%	☐ Pungent ___%	☐ Toasty ___%
☐ Herbal ___%	☐ Salty ___%	☐ ___ ___%
☐ Lactic ___%	☐ Sharp ___%	☐ ___ ___%

Rating

Appearance ☆☆☆☆☆   Comments: _____

Aroma ☆☆☆☆☆   _____

Taste ☆☆☆☆☆   _____

Overall Rating ☆☆☆☆☆   Buy Again: ○ Yes   ○ No

Name:

Origin: _____

Producer: _____

Age: _____ **Date :** _____

Price: _____

Milk

- ☐ Cow
- ☐ Sheep
- ☐ Goat
- ☐ Raw
- ☐ Other

_____
_____
_____

Texture

- ☐ Runny
- ☐ Soft
- ☐ Semi-soft
- ☐ Semi-firm
- ☐ Firm
- ☐ Hard

Notes

_____
_____
_____
_____
_____
_____
_____
_____
_____

Flavors

☐ Buttery ___%	☐ Lingering ___%	☐ Spicy ___%
☐ Grassy ___%	☐ Nutty ___%	☐ Sweet ___%
☐ Earthy ___%	☐ Pungent ___%	☐ Toasty ___%
☐ Herbal ___%	☐ Salty ___%	☐ _____ ___%
☐ Lactic ___%	☐ Sharp ___%	☐ _____ ___%

Rating

		Comments:
Appearance	☆☆☆☆☆	_____
Aroma	☆☆☆☆☆	_____
Taste	☆☆☆☆☆	_____

Overall Rating ☆☆☆☆☆　　**Buy Again:**　○ Yes　○ No

Name:

Origin: _____

Producer: _____

Age: _____ Date : _____

Price: _____

Milk

- ☐ Cow
- ☐ Sheep
- ☐ Goat
- ☐ Raw
- ☐ Other
  _____
  _____
  _____

Texture

- ☐ Runny
- ☐ Soft
- ☐ Semi-soft
- ☐ Semi-firm
- ☐ Firm
- ☐ Hard

Notes

_____
_____
_____
_____
_____
_____
_____
_____

Flavors

☐ Buttery ___%	☐ Lingering ___%	☐ Spicy ___%
☐ Grassy ___%	☐ Nutty ___%	☐ Sweet ___%
☐ Earthy ___%	☐ Pungent ___%	☐ Toasty ___%
☐ Herbal ___%	☐ Salty ___%	☐ ___ ___%
☐ Lactic ___%	☐ Sharp ___%	☐ ___ ___%

Rating

Appearance ☆☆☆☆☆   Comments: _____

Aroma ☆☆☆☆☆   _____

Taste ☆☆☆☆☆   _____

Overall Rating ☆☆☆☆☆   Buy Again: ○ Yes   ○ No

Name:

Origin: _____

Producer: _____

Age: _____ **Date :** _____

Price: _____

Milk

- ☐ Cow
- ☐ Sheep
- ☐ Goat
- ☐ Raw
- ☐ Other
- _____
- _____
- _____

Texture

- ☐ Runny
- ☐ Soft
- ☐ Semi-soft
- ☐ Semi-firm
- ☐ Firm
- ☐ Hard

Notes

_____
_____
_____
_____
_____
_____
_____
_____
_____

Flavors

- ☐ Buttery ___%
- ☐ Grassy ___%
- ☐ Earthy ___%
- ☐ Herbal ___%
- ☐ Lactic ___%

- ☐ Lingering ___%
- ☐ Nutty ___%
- ☐ Pungent ___%
- ☐ Salty ___%
- ☐ Sharp ___%

- ☐ Spicy ___%
- ☐ Sweet ___%
- ☐ Toasty ___%
- ☐ _____ ___%
- ☐ _____ ___%

Rating

Appearance	☆☆☆☆☆	Comments: _____
Aroma	☆☆☆☆☆	_____
Taste	☆☆☆☆☆	_____

Overall Rating ☆☆☆☆☆   **Buy Again:** ○ Yes   ○ No

Name:

Origin: _____

Producer: _____

Age: _____ Date : _____

Price: _____

Milk

- ☐ Cow
- ☐ Sheep
- ☐ Goat
- ☐ Raw
- ☐ Other
- _____
- _____
- _____

Texture

- ☐ Runny
- ☐ Soft
- ☐ Semi-soft
- ☐ Semi-firm
- ☐ Firm
- ☐ Hard

Notes

_____
_____
_____
_____
_____
_____
_____
_____
_____

Flavors

☐ Buttery ___%	☐ Lingering ___%	☐ Spicy ___%
☐ Grassy ___%	☐ Nutty ___%	☐ Sweet ___%
☐ Earthy ___%	☐ Pungent ___%	☐ Toasty ___%
☐ Herbal ___%	☐ Salty ___%	☐ ___ ___%
☐ Lactic ___%	☐ Sharp ___%	☐ ___ ___%

Rating

Appearance	☆☆☆☆☆	Comments: _____
Aroma	☆☆☆☆☆	_____
Taste	☆☆☆☆☆	_____

Overall Rating ☆☆☆☆☆   Buy Again: ◯ Yes   ◯ No

Name:

Origin: _____

Producer: _____

Age: _____ Date : _____

Price: _____

Milk

- ☐ Cow
- ☐ Sheep
- ☐ Goat
- ☐ Raw
- ☐ Other
- _____
- _____
- _____

Texture

- ☐ Runny
- ☐ Soft
- ☐ Semi-soft
- ☐ Semi-firm
- ☐ Firm
- ☐ Hard

Notes

_____
_____
_____
_____
_____
_____
_____
_____
_____

Flavors

☐ Buttery ___%	☐ Lingering ___%	☐ Spicy ___%
☐ Grassy ___%	☐ Nutty ___%	☐ Sweet ___%
☐ Earthy ___%	☐ Pungent ___%	☐ Toasty ___%
☐ Herbal ___%	☐ Salty ___%	☐ ___ ___%
☐ Lactic ___%	☐ Sharp ___%	☐ ___ ___%

Rating

Appearance	☆☆☆☆☆	Comments: _____
Aroma	☆☆☆☆☆	_____
Taste	☆☆☆☆☆	_____

Overall Rating ☆☆☆☆☆   Buy Again: ◯ Yes   ◯ No

Name:

Origin: _____

Producer: _____

Age: _____ Date : _____

Price: _____

Milk

- ☐ Cow
- ☐ Sheep
- ☐ Goat
- ☐ Raw
- ☐ Other

_____
_____
_____

Texture

- ☐ Runny
- ☐ Soft
- ☐ Semi-soft
- ☐ Semi-firm
- ☐ Firm
- ☐ Hard

Notes

_____
_____
_____
_____
_____
_____
_____
_____

Flavors

☐ Buttery __%	☐ Lingering __%	☐ Spicy __%
☐ Grassy __%	☐ Nutty __%	☐ Sweet __%
☐ Earthy __%	☐ Pungent __%	☐ Toasty __%
☐ Herbal __%	☐ Salty __%	☐ _____ __%
☐ Lactic __%	☐ Sharp __%	☐ _____ __%

Rating

Appearance ☆☆☆☆☆ Comments: _____

Aroma ☆☆☆☆☆ _____

Taste ☆☆☆☆☆ _____

Overall Rating ☆☆☆☆☆ Buy Again: ○ Yes ○ No

Name:

Origin: _____

Producer: _____

Age: _____ **Date :** _____

Price: _____

Milk

☐ Cow
☐ Sheep
☐ Goat
☐ Raw
☐ Other
_____
_____
_____

Texture

☐ Runny
☐ Soft
☐ Semi-soft
☐ Semi-firm
☐ Firm
☐ Hard

Notes

_____
_____
_____
_____
_____
_____
_____
_____
_____
_____

Flavors

☐ Buttery ___%	☐ Lingering ___%	☐ Spicy ___%
☐ Grassy ___%	☐ Nutty ___%	☐ Sweet ___%
☐ Earthy ___%	☐ Pungent ___%	☐ Toasty ___%
☐ Herbal ___%	☐ Salty ___%	☐ _____ ___%
☐ Lactic ___%	☐ Sharp ___%	☐ _____ ___%

Rating

Appearance ☆☆☆☆☆   Comments: _____

Aroma ☆☆☆☆☆   _____

Taste ☆☆☆☆☆   _____

Overall Rating ☆☆☆☆☆   Buy Again: ○ Yes   ○ No

Name:

Origin:_____

Producer:_____

Age:_____ Date : _____

Price:_____

Milk

- ☐ Cow
- ☐ Sheep
- ☐ Goat
- ☐ Raw
- ☐ Other

_____
_____
_____

Texture

- ☐ Runny
- ☐ Soft
- ☐ Semi-soft
- ☐ Semi-firm
- ☐ Firm
- ☐ Hard

Notes

_____
_____
_____
_____
_____
_____
_____
_____

Flavors

☐ Buttery ___%	☐ Lingering ___%	☐ Spicy ___%
☐ Grassy ___%	☐ Nutty ___%	☐ Sweet ___%
☐ Earthy ___%	☐ Pungent ___%	☐ Toasty ___%
☐ Herbal ___%	☐ Salty ___%	☐ _____ ___%
☐ Lactic ___%	☐ Sharp ___%	☐ _____ ___%

Rating

Appearance ☆☆☆☆☆   Comments:_____

Aroma ☆☆☆☆☆   _____

Taste ☆☆☆☆☆   _____

Overall Rating ☆☆☆☆☆   Buy Again: ○ Yes   ○ No

Name:

Origin: _____

Producer: _____

Age: _____ **Date :** _____

Price: _____

Milk

- ☐ Cow
- ☐ Sheep
- ☐ Goat
- ☐ Raw
- ☐ Other
- _____
- _____
- _____

Texture

- ☐ Runny
- ☐ Soft
- ☐ Semi-soft
- ☐ Semi-firm
- ☐ Firm
- ☐ Hard

Notes

_____
_____
_____
_____
_____
_____
_____
_____
_____
_____

Flavors

☐ Buttery ___%	☐ Lingering ___%	☐ Spicy ___%
☐ Grassy ___%	☐ Nutty ___%	☐ Sweet ___%
☐ Earthy ___%	☐ Pungent ___%	☐ Toasty ___%
☐ Herbal ___%	☐ Salty ___%	☐ ____ ___%
☐ Lactic ___%	☐ Sharp ___%	☐ ____ ___%

Rating

Appearance	☆☆☆☆☆	Comments: _____
Aroma	☆☆☆☆☆	_____
Taste	☆☆☆☆☆	_____

Overall Rating ☆☆☆☆☆ **Buy Again:** ◯ Yes ◯ No

Name:

Origin: _____

Producer: _____

Age: _____ Date : _____

Price: _____

Milk

☐ Cow
☐ Sheep
☐ Goat
☐ Raw
☐ Other
_____
_____
_____

Texture

☐ Runny
☐ Soft
☐ Semi-soft
☐ Semi-firm
☐ Firm
☐ Hard

Notes

_____
_____
_____
_____
_____
_____
_____
_____
_____

Flavors

☐ Buttery ____%	☐ Lingering ____%	☐ Spicy ____%
☐ Grassy ____%	☐ Nutty ____%	☐ Sweet ____%
☐ Earthy ____%	☐ Pungent ____%	☐ Toasty ____%
☐ Herbal ____%	☐ Salty ____%	☐ _____ ____%
☐ Lactic ____%	☐ Sharp ____%	☐ _____ ____%

Rating

Appearance ☆☆☆☆☆   Comments: _____
Aroma ☆☆☆☆☆   _____
Taste ☆☆☆☆☆   _____

Overall Rating ☆☆☆☆☆   Buy Again: ○ Yes   ○ No

Name:

Origin:_____

Producer:_____

Age:_____ Date :_____

Price:_____

Milk

- ☐ Cow
- ☐ Sheep
- ☐ Goat
- ☐ Raw
- ☐ Other
- _____
- _____
- _____

Texture

- ☐ Runny
- ☐ Soft
- ☐ Semi-soft
- ☐ Semi-firm
- ☐ Firm
- ☐ Hard

Notes

_____
_____
_____
_____
_____
_____
_____
_____

Flavors

☐ Buttery ___%	☐ Lingering ___%	☐ Spicy ___%
☐ Grassy ___%	☐ Nutty ___%	☐ Sweet ___%
☐ Earthy ___%	☐ Pungent ___%	☐ Toasty ___%
☐ Herbal ___%	☐ Salty ___%	☐ _____ ___%
☐ Lactic ___%	☐ Sharp ___%	☐ _____ ___%

Rating

Appearance ☆☆☆☆☆   Comments:_____

Aroma ☆☆☆☆☆   _____

Taste ☆☆☆☆☆   _____

Overall Rating ☆☆☆☆☆   Buy Again: ○ Yes   ○ No

Name:

Origin:_____

Producer:_____

Age:_____ Date :_____

Price:_____

Milk

- ☐ Cow
- ☐ Sheep
- ☐ Goat
- ☐ Raw
- ☐ Other
- _____
- _____
- _____

Texture

- ☐ Runny
- ☐ Soft
- ☐ Semi-soft
- ☐ Semi-firm
- ☐ Firm
- ☐ Hard

Notes

_____
_____
_____
_____
_____
_____
_____
_____
_____

Flavors

☐ Buttery ___%	☐ Lingering ___%	☐ Spicy ___%
☐ Grassy ___%	☐ Nutty ___%	☐ Sweet ___%
☐ Earthy ___%	☐ Pungent ___%	☐ Toasty ___%
☐ Herbal ___%	☐ Salty ___%	☐ ____ ___%
☐ Lactic ___%	☐ Sharp ___%	☐ ____ ___%

Rating

Appearance	☆☆☆☆☆	Comments:_____
Aroma	☆☆☆☆☆	_____
Taste	☆☆☆☆☆	_____

Overall Rating ☆☆☆☆☆   Buy Again: ◯ Yes   ◯ No

Name:

Origin: _____

Producer: _____

Age: _____ Date : _____

Price: _____

Milk

- ☐ Cow
- ☐ Sheep
- ☐ Goat
- ☐ Raw
- ☐ Other
- _____
- _____
- _____

Texture

- ☐ Runny
- ☐ Soft
- ☐ Semi-soft
- ☐ Semi-firm
- ☐ Firm
- ☐ Hard

Notes

_____
_____
_____
_____
_____
_____
_____
_____

Flavors

☐ Buttery ___%	☐ Lingering ___%	☐ Spicy ___%
☐ Grassy ___%	☐ Nutty ___%	☐ Sweet ___%
☐ Earthy ___%	☐ Pungent ___%	☐ Toasty ___%
☐ Herbal ___%	☐ Salty ___%	☐ ___ ___%
☐ Lactic ___%	☐ Sharp ___%	☐ ___ ___%

Rating

Appearance ☆☆☆☆☆	Comments: _____
Aroma ☆☆☆☆☆	_____
Taste ☆☆☆☆☆	_____

Overall Rating ☆☆☆☆☆   Buy Again: ○ Yes   ○ No

Name:

Origin: _____

Producer: _____

Age: _____ Date : _____

Price: _____

Milk

- ☐ Cow
- ☐ Sheep
- ☐ Goat
- ☐ Raw
- ☐ Other

_____
_____
_____

Texture

- ☐ Runny
- ☐ Soft
- ☐ Semi-soft
- ☐ Semi-firm
- ☐ Firm
- ☐ Hard

Notes

_____
_____
_____
_____
_____
_____
_____
_____

Flavors

- ☐ Buttery ___%
- ☐ Grassy ___%
- ☐ Earthy ___%
- ☐ Herbal ___%
- ☐ Lactic ___%

- ☐ Lingering ___%
- ☐ Nutty ___%
- ☐ Pungent ___%
- ☐ Salty ___%
- ☐ Sharp ___%

- ☐ Spicy ___%
- ☐ Sweet ___%
- ☐ Toasty ___%
- ☐ _____ ___%
- ☐ _____ ___%

Rating

Appearance ☆☆☆☆☆
Aroma ☆☆☆☆☆
Taste ☆☆☆☆☆

Comments: _____
_____
_____

Overall Rating ☆☆☆☆☆   Buy Again: ○ Yes   ○ No

Name:

Origin: _____

Producer: _____

Age: _____ Date : _____

Price: _____

Milk

- ☐ Cow
- ☐ Sheep
- ☐ Goat
- ☐ Raw
- ☐ Other
- _____
- _____
- _____

Texture

- ☐ Runny
- ☐ Soft
- ☐ Semi-soft
- ☐ Semi-firm
- ☐ Firm
- ☐ Hard

Notes

_____
_____
_____
_____
_____
_____
_____
_____

Flavors

☐ Buttery ___%	☐ Lingering ___%	☐ Spicy ___%
☐ Grassy ___%	☐ Nutty ___%	☐ Sweet ___%
☐ Earthy ___%	☐ Pungent ___%	☐ Toasty ___%
☐ Herbal ___%	☐ Salty ___%	☐ _____ ___%
☐ Lactic ___%	☐ Sharp ___%	☐ _____ ___%

Rating

Appearance ☆☆☆☆☆   Comments: _____

Aroma ☆☆☆☆☆   _____

Taste ☆☆☆☆☆   _____

Overall Rating ☆☆☆☆☆   Buy Again: ○ Yes   ○ No

Name:

Origin: _____

Producer: _____

Age: _____ Date : _____

Price: _____

Milk

- ☐ Cow
- ☐ Sheep
- ☐ Goat
- ☐ Raw
- ☐ Other

_____
_____
_____

Texture

- ☐ Runny
- ☐ Soft
- ☐ Semi-soft
- ☐ Semi-firm
- ☐ Firm
- ☐ Hard

Notes

_____
_____
_____
_____
_____
_____
_____
_____

Flavors

☐ Buttery ___%	☐ Lingering ___%	☐ Spicy ___%
☐ Grassy ___%	☐ Nutty ___%	☐ Sweet ___%
☐ Earthy ___%	☐ Pungent ___%	☐ Toasty ___%
☐ Herbal ___%	☐ Salty ___%	☐ _____ ___%
☐ Lactic ___%	☐ Sharp ___%	☐ _____ ___%

Rating

Appearance	☆☆☆☆☆	Comments: _____
Aroma	☆☆☆☆☆	_____
Taste	☆☆☆☆☆	_____

Overall Rating ☆☆☆☆☆   Buy Again: ◯ Yes   ◯ No

Name:

Origin: _____

Producer: _____

Age: _____ Date : _____

Price: _____

Milk

- ☐ Cow
- ☐ Sheep
- ☐ Goat
- ☐ Raw
- ☐ Other
- _____
- _____
- _____

Texture

- ☐ Runny
- ☐ Soft
- ☐ Semi-soft
- ☐ Semi-firm
- ☐ Firm
- ☐ Hard

Notes

_____
_____
_____
_____
_____
_____
_____
_____
_____

Flavors

☐ Buttery ___%	☐ Lingering ___%	☐ Spicy ___%
☐ Grassy ___%	☐ Nutty ___%	☐ Sweet ___%
☐ Earthy ___%	☐ Pungent ___%	☐ Toasty ___%
☐ Herbal ___%	☐ Salty ___%	☐ _____ ___%
☐ Lactic ___%	☐ Sharp ___%	☐ _____ ___%

Rating

Appearance	☆☆☆☆☆	Comments: _____
Aroma	☆☆☆☆☆	_____
Taste	☆☆☆☆☆	_____

Overall Rating ☆☆☆☆☆   Buy Again: ○ Yes   ○ No

Name:

Origin: _____

Producer: _____

Age: _____ Date : _____

Price: _____

Milk

- ☐ Cow
- ☐ Sheep
- ☐ Goat
- ☐ Raw
- ☐ Other
- _____
- _____
- _____

Texture

- ☐ Runny
- ☐ Soft
- ☐ Semi-soft
- ☐ Semi-firm
- ☐ Firm
- ☐ Hard

Notes

_____
_____
_____
_____
_____
_____
_____
_____
_____

Flavors

☐ Buttery ___%	☐ Lingering ___%	☐ Spicy ___%
☐ Grassy ___%	☐ Nutty ___%	☐ Sweet ___%
☐ Earthy ___%	☐ Pungent ___%	☐ Toasty ___%
☐ Herbal ___%	☐ Salty ___%	☐ _____ ___%
☐ Lactic ___%	☐ Sharp ___%	☐ _____ ___%

Rating

Appearance	☆☆☆☆☆	Comments: _____
Aroma	☆☆☆☆☆	_____
Taste	☆☆☆☆☆	_____

Overall Rating ☆☆☆☆☆   Buy Again: ◯ Yes   ◯ No

Name:

Origin:_____

Producer:_____

Age:_____ Date :_____

Price:_____

Milk

- ☐ Cow
- ☐ Sheep
- ☐ Goat
- ☐ Raw
- ☐ Other
- _____
- _____
- _____

Texture

- ☐ Runny
- ☐ Soft
- ☐ Semi-soft
- ☐ Semi-firm
- ☐ Firm
- ☐ Hard

Notes

_____
_____
_____
_____
_____
_____
_____
_____
_____
_____

Flavors

☐ Buttery ___%	☐ Lingering ___%	☐ Spicy ___%
☐ Grassy ___%	☐ Nutty ___%	☐ Sweet ___%
☐ Earthy ___%	☐ Pungent ___%	☐ Toasty ___%
☐ Herbal ___%	☐ Salty ___%	☐ ___ ___%
☐ Lactic ___%	☐ Sharp ___%	☐ ___ ___%

Rating

Appearance	☆☆☆☆☆	Comments:_____
Aroma	☆☆☆☆☆	_____
Taste	☆☆☆☆☆	_____

Overall Rating ☆☆☆☆☆   Buy Again: ◯ Yes   ◯ No

Name:

Origin: _____

Producer: _____

Age: _____ **Date :** _____

Price: _____

Milk

- ☐ Cow
- ☐ Sheep
- ☐ Goat
- ☐ Raw
- ☐ Other
- _____
- _____
- _____

Texture

- ☐ Runny
- ☐ Soft
- ☐ Semi-soft
- ☐ Semi-firm
- ☐ Firm
- ☐ Hard

Notes

_____
_____
_____
_____
_____
_____
_____
_____
_____

Flavors

☐ Buttery ___%	☐ Lingering ___%	☐ Spicy ___%
☐ Grassy ___%	☐ Nutty ___%	☐ Sweet ___%
☐ Earthy ___%	☐ Pungent ___%	☐ Toasty ___%
☐ Herbal ___%	☐ Salty ___%	☐ ___ ___%
☐ Lactic ___%	☐ Sharp ___%	☐ ___ ___%

Rating

Appearance	☆☆☆☆☆	Comments: _____
Aroma	☆☆☆☆☆	_____
Taste	☆☆☆☆☆	_____

Overall Rating ☆☆☆☆☆ **Buy Again:** ◯ Yes ◯ No

Name:

Origin: _____

Producer: _____

Age: _____ Date : _____

Price: _____

Milk

- ☐ Cow
- ☐ Sheep
- ☐ Goat
- ☐ Raw
- ☐ Other
- _____
- _____
- _____

Texture

- ☐ Runny
- ☐ Soft
- ☐ Semi-soft
- ☐ Semi-firm
- ☐ Firm
- ☐ Hard

Notes

_____

_____

_____

_____

_____

_____

_____

_____

_____

Flavors

- ☐ Buttery ___%
- ☐ Grassy ___%
- ☐ Earthy ___%
- ☐ Herbal ___%
- ☐ Lactic ___%

- ☐ Lingering ___%
- ☐ Nutty ___%
- ☐ Pungent ___%
- ☐ Salty ___%
- ☐ Sharp ___%

- ☐ Spicy ___%
- ☐ Sweet ___%
- ☐ Toasty ___%
- ☐ _____ ___%
- ☐ _____ ___%

Rating

Appearance ☆☆☆☆☆   Comments: _____

Aroma ☆☆☆☆☆   _____

Taste ☆☆☆☆☆   _____

Overall Rating ☆☆☆☆☆   Buy Again: ◯ Yes   ◯ No

Name:

Origin: _____

Producer: _____

Age: _____ Date : _____

Price: _____

Milk

- ☐ Cow
- ☐ Sheep
- ☐ Goat
- ☐ Raw
- ☐ Other
- _____
- _____
- _____

Texture

- ☐ Runny
- ☐ Soft
- ☐ Semi-soft
- ☐ Semi-firm
- ☐ Firm
- ☐ Hard

Notes

_____
_____
_____
_____
_____
_____
_____
_____
_____

Flavors

☐ Buttery ___%	☐ Lingering ___%	☐ Spicy ___%
☐ Grassy ___%	☐ Nutty ___%	☐ Sweet ___%
☐ Earthy ___%	☐ Pungent ___%	☐ Toasty ___%
☐ Herbal ___%	☐ Salty ___%	☐ _____ ___%
☐ Lactic ___%	☐ Sharp ___%	☐ _____ ___%

Rating

Appearance	☆☆☆☆☆	Comments: _____
Aroma	☆☆☆☆☆	_____
Taste	☆☆☆☆☆	_____

Overall Rating ☆☆☆☆☆   Buy Again: ○ Yes   ○ No

Name:

Origin: _____

Producer: _____

Age: _____ Date : _____

Price: _____

Milk

- ☐ Cow
- ☐ Sheep
- ☐ Goat
- ☐ Raw
- ☐ Other

_____

_____

_____

Texture

- ☐ Runny
- ☐ Soft
- ☐ Semi-soft
- ☐ Semi-firm
- ☐ Firm
- ☐ Hard

Notes

_____

_____

_____

_____

_____

_____

_____

_____

_____

Flavors

☐ Buttery ___%	☐ Lingering ___%	☐ Spicy ___%
☐ Grassy ___%	☐ Nutty ___%	☐ Sweet ___%
☐ Earthy ___%	☐ Pungent ___%	☐ Toasty ___%
☐ Herbal ___%	☐ Salty ___%	☐ _____ ___%
☐ Lactic ___%	☐ Sharp ___%	☐ _____ ___%

Rating

Appearance	☆☆☆☆☆	Comments: _____
Aroma	☆☆☆☆☆	_____
Taste	☆☆☆☆☆	_____

Overall Rating ☆☆☆☆☆   Buy Again: ○ Yes   ○ No

Name:

Origin: _____

Producer: _____

Age: _____ Date : _____

Price: _____

Milk

- ☐ Cow
- ☐ Sheep
- ☐ Goat
- ☐ Raw
- ☐ Other
- _____
- _____
- _____

Texture

- ☐ Runny
- ☐ Soft
- ☐ Semi-soft
- ☐ Semi-firm
- ☐ Firm
- ☐ Hard

Notes

_____
_____
_____
_____
_____
_____
_____
_____

Flavors

☐ Buttery ___%	☐ Lingering ___%	☐ Spicy ___%
☐ Grassy ___%	☐ Nutty ___%	☐ Sweet ___%
☐ Earthy ___%	☐ Pungent ___%	☐ Toasty ___%
☐ Herbal ___%	☐ Salty ___%	☐ _____ ___%
☐ Lactic ___%	☐ Sharp ___%	☐ _____ ___%

Rating

Appearance ☆☆☆☆☆   Comments: _____

Aroma ☆☆☆☆☆   _____

Taste ☆☆☆☆☆   _____

Overall Rating ☆☆☆☆☆   Buy Again: ○ Yes   ○ No

Name:

Origin: _____

Producer: _____

Age: _____ **Date :** _____

Price: _____

Milk

- ☐ Cow
- ☐ Sheep
- ☐ Goat
- ☐ Raw
- ☐ Other
- _____
- _____
- _____

Texture

- ☐ Runny
- ☐ Soft
- ☐ Semi-soft
- ☐ Semi-firm
- ☐ Firm
- ☐ Hard

Notes

_____
_____
_____
_____
_____
_____
_____
_____

Flavors

☐ Buttery ___%	☐ Lingering ___%	☐ Spicy ___%
☐ Grassy ___%	☐ Nutty ___%	☐ Sweet ___%
☐ Earthy ___%	☐ Pungent ___%	☐ Toasty ___%
☐ Herbal ___%	☐ Salty ___%	☐ _____ ___%
☐ Lactic ___%	☐ Sharp ___%	☐ _____ ___%

Rating

Appearance	☆☆☆☆☆	Comments: _____
Aroma	☆☆☆☆☆	_____
Taste	☆☆☆☆☆	_____

Overall Rating ☆☆☆☆☆   **Buy Again:**   ○ Yes   ○ No

Name:

Origin: _____

Producer: _____

Age: _____ **Date :** _____

Price: _____

Milk

- ☐ Cow
- ☐ Sheep
- ☐ Goat
- ☐ Raw
- ☐ Other
- _____
- _____
- _____

Texture

- ☐ Runny
- ☐ Soft
- ☐ Semi-soft
- ☐ Semi-firm
- ☐ Firm
- ☐ Hard

Notes

_____
_____
_____
_____
_____
_____
_____
_____

Flavors

☐ Buttery ___%	☐ Lingering ___%	☐ Spicy ___%
☐ Grassy ___%	☐ Nutty ___%	☐ Sweet ___%
☐ Earthy ___%	☐ Pungent ___%	☐ Toasty ___%
☐ Herbal ___%	☐ Salty ___%	☐ _____ ___%
☐ Lactic ___%	☐ Sharp ___%	☐ _____ ___%

Rating

Appearance	☆☆☆☆☆	Comments: _____
Aroma	☆☆☆☆☆	_____
Taste	☆☆☆☆☆	_____

Overall Rating ☆☆☆☆☆   **Buy Again:** ○ Yes   ○ No

Name:

Origin: _____

Producer: _____

Age: _____ Date : _____

Price: _____

Milk

- ☐ Cow
- ☐ Sheep
- ☐ Goat
- ☐ Raw
- ☐ Other
- _____
- _____
- _____

Texture

- ☐ Runny
- ☐ Soft
- ☐ Semi-soft
- ☐ Semi-firm
- ☐ Firm
- ☐ Hard

Notes

_____
_____
_____
_____
_____
_____
_____
_____
_____
_____

Flavors

☐ Buttery ___%	☐ Lingering ___%	☐ Spicy ___%
☐ Grassy ___%	☐ Nutty ___%	☐ Sweet ___%
☐ Earthy ___%	☐ Pungent ___%	☐ Toasty ___%
☐ Herbal ___%	☐ Salty ___%	☐ ___ ___%
☐ Lactic ___%	☐ Sharp ___%	☐ ___ ___%

Rating

Appearance	☆☆☆☆☆	Comments: _____
Aroma	☆☆☆☆☆	_____
Taste	☆☆☆☆☆	_____

Overall Rating ☆☆☆☆☆ Buy Again: ○ Yes ○ No

Name:

Origin: _____

Producer: _____

Age: _____ Date : _____

Price: _____

Milk
- ☐ Cow
- ☐ Sheep
- ☐ Goat
- ☐ Raw
- ☐ Other
- _____
- _____
- _____

Texture
- ☐ Runny
- ☐ Soft
- ☐ Semi-soft
- ☐ Semi-firm
- ☐ Firm
- ☐ Hard

Notes
_____
_____
_____
_____
_____
_____
_____
_____

Flavors
☐ Buttery ___%	☐ Lingering ___%	☐ Spicy ___%
☐ Grassy ___%	☐ Nutty ___%	☐ Sweet ___%
☐ Earthy ___%	☐ Pungent ___%	☐ Toasty ___%
☐ Herbal ___%	☐ Salty ___%	☐ _____ ___%
☐ Lactic ___%	☐ Sharp ___%	☐ _____ ___%

Rating

Appearance ☆☆☆☆☆   Comments: _____

Aroma ☆☆☆☆☆   _____

Taste ☆☆☆☆☆   _____

Overall Rating ☆☆☆☆☆   Buy Again: ○ Yes   ○ No

Name:

Origin: _____

Producer: _____

Age: _____ Date : _____

Price: _____

Milk

- ☐ Cow
- ☐ Sheep
- ☐ Goat
- ☐ Raw
- ☐ Other
- _____
- _____
- _____

Texture

- ☐ Runny
- ☐ Soft
- ☐ Semi-soft
- ☐ Semi-firm
- ☐ Firm
- ☐ Hard

Notes

_____
_____
_____
_____
_____
_____
_____
_____
_____

Flavors

☐ Buttery ___%	☐ Lingering ___%	☐ Spicy ___%
☐ Grassy ___%	☐ Nutty ___%	☐ Sweet ___%
☐ Earthy ___%	☐ Pungent ___%	☐ Toasty ___%
☐ Herbal ___%	☐ Salty ___%	☐ ___ ___%
☐ Lactic ___%	☐ Sharp ___%	☐ ___ ___%

Rating

		Comments:
Appearance	☆☆☆☆☆	_____
Aroma	☆☆☆☆☆	_____
Taste	☆☆☆☆☆	_____

Overall Rating ☆☆☆☆☆   Buy Again: ○ Yes   ○ No

Name:

Origin: _____

Producer: _____

Age: _____ Date : _____

Price: _____

Milk

- ☐ Cow
- ☐ Sheep
- ☐ Goat
- ☐ Raw
- ☐ Other
- _____
- _____
- _____

Texture

- ☐ Runny
- ☐ Soft
- ☐ Semi-soft
- ☐ Semi-firm
- ☐ Firm
- ☐ Hard

Notes

_____
_____
_____
_____
_____
_____
_____
_____
_____

Flavors

☐ Buttery ___%	☐ Lingering ___%	☐ Spicy ___%
☐ Grassy ___%	☐ Nutty ___%	☐ Sweet ___%
☐ Earthy ___%	☐ Pungent ___%	☐ Toasty ___%
☐ Herbal ___%	☐ Salty ___%	☐ _____ ___%
☐ Lactic ___%	☐ Sharp ___%	☐ _____ ___%

Rating

Appearance ☆☆☆☆☆	Comments: _____
Aroma ☆☆☆☆☆	_____
Taste ☆☆☆☆☆	_____

Overall Rating ☆☆☆☆☆   Buy Again: ○ Yes   ○ No

Name:

Origin: _____

Producer: _____

Age: _____ Date: _____

Price: _____

Milk

- ☐ Cow
- ☐ Sheep
- ☐ Goat
- ☐ Raw
- ☐ Other
- _____
- _____
- _____

Texture

- ☐ Runny
- ☐ Soft
- ☐ Semi-soft
- ☐ Semi-firm
- ☐ Firm
- ☐ Hard

Notes

_____
_____
_____
_____
_____
_____
_____
_____

Flavors

☐ Buttery ___%	☐ Lingering ___%	☐ Spicy ___%
☐ Grassy ___%	☐ Nutty ___%	☐ Sweet ___%
☐ Earthy ___%	☐ Pungent ___%	☐ Toasty ___%
☐ Herbal ___%	☐ Salty ___%	☐ ___ ___%
☐ Lactic ___%	☐ Sharp ___%	☐ ___ ___%

Rating

Appearance	☆☆☆☆☆	Comments: _____
Aroma	☆☆☆☆☆	_____
Taste	☆☆☆☆☆	_____

Overall Rating ☆☆☆☆☆　　Buy Again: ○ Yes　○ No

Name:

Origin: _____

Producer: _____

Age: _____ Date : _____

Price: _____

Milk

- ☐ Cow
- ☐ Sheep
- ☐ Goat
- ☐ Raw
- ☐ Other
_____
_____
_____

Texture

- ☐ Runny
- ☐ Soft
- ☐ Semi-soft
- ☐ Semi-firm
- ☐ Firm
- ☐ Hard

Notes

_____
_____
_____
_____
_____
_____
_____
_____

Flavors

☐ Buttery ___%	☐ Lingering ___%	☐ Spicy ___%
☐ Grassy ___%	☐ Nutty ___%	☐ Sweet ___%
☐ Earthy ___%	☐ Pungent ___%	☐ Toasty ___%
☐ Herbal ___%	☐ Salty ___%	☐ ___ ___%
☐ Lactic ___%	☐ Sharp ___%	☐ ___ ___%

Rating

Appearance	☆☆☆☆☆	Comments: _____
Aroma	☆☆☆☆☆	_____
Taste	☆☆☆☆☆	_____

Overall Rating ☆☆☆☆☆   Buy Again: ○ Yes   ○ No

Name:

Origin: _____

Producer: _____

Age: _____ Date : _____

Price: _____

Milk

- ☐ Cow
- ☐ Sheep
- ☐ Goat
- ☐ Raw
- ☐ Other
- _____
- _____
- _____

Texture

- ☐ Runny
- ☐ Soft
- ☐ Semi-soft
- ☐ Semi-firm
- ☐ Firm
- ☐ Hard

Notes

_____
_____
_____
_____
_____
_____
_____
_____
_____

Flavors

☐ Buttery ___%	☐ Lingering ___%	☐ Spicy ___%
☐ Grassy ___%	☐ Nutty ___%	☐ Sweet ___%
☐ Earthy ___%	☐ Pungent ___%	☐ Toasty ___%
☐ Herbal ___%	☐ Salty ___%	☐ _____ ___%
☐ Lactic ___%	☐ Sharp ___%	☐ _____ ___%

Rating

Appearance	☆☆☆☆☆	Comments: _____
Aroma	☆☆☆☆☆	_____
Taste	☆☆☆☆☆	_____

Overall Rating ☆☆☆☆☆   Buy Again: ○ Yes   ○ No

Name:

Origin: _____

Producer: _____

Age: _____ Date : _____

Price: _____

Milk

- ☐ Cow
- ☐ Sheep
- ☐ Goat
- ☐ Raw
- ☐ Other

_____
_____
_____

Texture

- ☐ Runny
- ☐ Soft
- ☐ Semi-soft
- ☐ Semi-firm
- ☐ Firm
- ☐ Hard

Notes

_____
_____
_____
_____
_____
_____
_____
_____
_____

Flavors

☐ Buttery ___%	☐ Lingering ___%	☐ Spicy ___%
☐ Grassy ___%	☐ Nutty ___%	☐ Sweet ___%
☐ Earthy ___%	☐ Pungent ___%	☐ Toasty ___%
☐ Herbal ___%	☐ Salty ___%	☐ _____ ___%
☐ Lactic ___%	☐ Sharp ___%	☐ _____ ___%

Rating

Appearance ☆☆☆☆☆

Aroma ☆☆☆☆☆

Taste ☆☆☆☆☆

Comments: _____
_____
_____

Overall Rating ☆☆☆☆☆   Buy Again: ○ Yes   ○ No

Name:

Origin: _____

Producer: _____

Age: _____ Date : _____

Price: _____

Milk

- ☐ Cow
- ☐ Sheep
- ☐ Goat
- ☐ Raw
- ☐ Other

_____
_____
_____

Texture

- ☐ Runny
- ☐ Soft
- ☐ Semi-soft
- ☐ Semi-firm
- ☐ Firm
- ☐ Hard

Notes

_____
_____
_____
_____
_____
_____
_____
_____
_____

Flavors

☐ Buttery ___%	☐ Lingering ___%	☐ Spicy ___%
☐ Grassy ___%	☐ Nutty ___%	☐ Sweet ___%
☐ Earthy ___%	☐ Pungent ___%	☐ Toasty ___%
☐ Herbal ___%	☐ Salty ___%	☐ _____ ___%
☐ Lactic ___%	☐ Sharp ___%	☐ _____ ___%

Rating

Appearance	☆☆☆☆☆	Comments: _____
Aroma	☆☆☆☆☆	_____
Taste	☆☆☆☆☆	_____

Overall Rating ☆☆☆☆☆   Buy Again: ○ Yes   ○ No

Name:

Origin: _____

Producer: _____

Age: _____ Date : _____

Price: _____

Milk

- ☐ Cow
- ☐ Sheep
- ☐ Goat
- ☐ Raw
- ☐ Other
- _____
- _____
- _____

Texture

- ☐ Runny
- ☐ Soft
- ☐ Semi-soft
- ☐ Semi-firm
- ☐ Firm
- ☐ Hard

Notes

_____
_____
_____
_____
_____
_____
_____
_____
_____

Flavors

- ☐ Buttery ___%
- ☐ Grassy ___%
- ☐ Earthy ___%
- ☐ Herbal ___%
- ☐ Lactic ___%

- ☐ Lingering ___%
- ☐ Nutty ___%
- ☐ Pungent ___%
- ☐ Salty ___%
- ☐ Sharp ___%

- ☐ Spicy ___%
- ☐ Sweet ___%
- ☐ Toasty ___%
- ☐ _____ ___%
- ☐ _____ ___%

Rating

Appearance ☆☆☆☆☆   Comments: _____

Aroma ☆☆☆☆☆   _____

Taste ☆☆☆☆☆   _____

Overall Rating ☆☆☆☆☆   Buy Again: ◯ Yes   ◯ No

Name:

Origin: _____

Producer: _____

Age: _____ **Date :** _____

Price: _____

Milk

- ☐ Cow
- ☐ Sheep
- ☐ Goat
- ☐ Raw
- ☐ Other
- _____
- _____
- _____

Texture

- ☐ Runny
- ☐ Soft
- ☐ Semi-soft
- ☐ Semi-firm
- ☐ Firm
- ☐ Hard

Notes

_____
_____
_____
_____
_____
_____
_____
_____
_____

Flavors

☐ Buttery ___%	☐ Lingering ___%	☐ Spicy ___%
☐ Grassy ___%	☐ Nutty ___%	☐ Sweet ___%
☐ Earthy ___%	☐ Pungent ___%	☐ Toasty ___%
☐ Herbal ___%	☐ Salty ___%	☐ _____ ___%
☐ Lactic ___%	☐ Sharp ___%	☐ _____ ___%

Rating

Appearance	☆☆☆☆☆	Comments: _____
Aroma	☆☆☆☆☆	_____
Taste	☆☆☆☆☆	_____

Overall Rating ☆☆☆☆☆ **Buy Again:** ◯ Yes ◯ No

Name:

Origin: _____

Producer: _____

Age: _____ Date : _____

Price: _____

Milk

- ☐ Cow
- ☐ Sheep
- ☐ Goat
- ☐ Raw
- ☐ Other
  _____
  _____
  _____

Texture

- ☐ Runny
- ☐ Soft
- ☐ Semi-soft
- ☐ Semi-firm
- ☐ Firm
- ☐ Hard

Notes

_____
_____
_____
_____
_____
_____
_____
_____

Flavors

☐ Buttery ___%	☐ Lingering ___%	☐ Spicy ___%
☐ Grassy ___%	☐ Nutty ___%	☐ Sweet ___%
☐ Earthy ___%	☐ Pungent ___%	☐ Toasty ___%
☐ Herbal ___%	☐ Salty ___%	☐ _____ ___%
☐ Lactic ___%	☐ Sharp ___%	☐ _____ ___%

Rating

Appearance	☆☆☆☆☆	Comments: _____
Aroma	☆☆☆☆☆	_____
Taste	☆☆☆☆☆	_____

Overall Rating ☆☆☆☆☆   Buy Again: ○ Yes   ○ No

Name:

Origin: _____

Producer: _____

Age: _____ Date : _____

Price: _____

Milk

☐ Cow
☐ Sheep
☐ Goat
☐ Raw
☐ Other
_____
_____
_____

Texture

☐ Runny
☐ Soft
☐ Semi-soft
☐ Semi-firm
☐ Firm
☐ Hard

Notes

_____
_____
_____
_____
_____
_____
_____
_____
_____
_____

Flavors

☐ Buttery ___%	☐ Lingering ___%	☐ Spicy ___%
☐ Grassy ___%	☐ Nutty ___%	☐ Sweet ___%
☐ Earthy ___%	☐ Pungent ___%	☐ Toasty ___%
☐ Herbal ___%	☐ Salty ___%	☐ _____ ___%
☐ Lactic ___%	☐ Sharp ___%	☐ _____ ___%

Rating

Appearance ☆☆☆☆☆   Comments: _____
Aroma ☆☆☆☆☆   _____
Taste ☆☆☆☆☆   _____

Overall Rating ☆☆☆☆☆   Buy Again: ◯ Yes   ◯ No

Name:

Origin: _____

Producer: _____

Age: _____ Date : _____

Price: _____

Milk

- ☐ Cow
- ☐ Sheep
- ☐ Goat
- ☐ Raw
- ☐ Other

_____
_____
_____

Texture

- ☐ Runny
- ☐ Soft
- ☐ Semi-soft
- ☐ Semi-firm
- ☐ Firm
- ☐ Hard

Notes

_____
_____
_____
_____
_____
_____
_____
_____

Flavors

☐ Buttery ___%	☐ Lingering ___%	☐ Spicy ___%
☐ Grassy ___%	☐ Nutty ___%	☐ Sweet ___%
☐ Earthy ___%	☐ Pungent ___%	☐ Toasty ___%
☐ Herbal ___%	☐ Salty ___%	☐ _____ ___%
☐ Lactic ___%	☐ Sharp ___%	☐ _____ ___%

Rating

Appearance ☆☆☆☆☆	Comments: _____
Aroma ☆☆☆☆☆	_____
Taste ☆☆☆☆☆	_____

Overall Rating ☆☆☆☆☆   Buy Again: ○ Yes   ○ No

Name:

Origin: _____

Producer: _____

Age: _____ Date : _____

Price: _____

Milk

- ☐ Cow
- ☐ Sheep
- ☐ Goat
- ☐ Raw
- ☐ Other

_____
_____
_____

Texture

- ☐ Runny
- ☐ Soft
- ☐ Semi-soft
- ☐ Semi-firm
- ☐ Firm
- ☐ Hard

Notes

_____
_____
_____
_____
_____
_____
_____
_____
_____

Flavors

☐ Buttery ___%	☐ Lingering ___%	☐ Spicy ___%
☐ Grassy ___%	☐ Nutty ___%	☐ Sweet ___%
☐ Earthy ___%	☐ Pungent ___%	☐ Toasty ___%
☐ Herbal ___%	☐ Salty ___%	☐ _____ ___%
☐ Lactic ___%	☐ Sharp ___%	☐ _____ ___%

Rating

Appearance	☆☆☆☆☆	Comments: _____
Aroma	☆☆☆☆☆	_____
Taste	☆☆☆☆☆	_____

Overall Rating ☆☆☆☆☆   Buy Again: ◯ Yes   ◯ No

Name:

Origin: _____

Producer: _____

Age: _____ Date : _____

Price: _____

Milk

- ☐ Cow
- ☐ Sheep
- ☐ Goat
- ☐ Raw
- ☐ Other

_____
_____
_____

Texture

- ☐ Runny
- ☐ Soft
- ☐ Semi-soft
- ☐ Semi-firm
- ☐ Firm
- ☐ Hard

Notes

_____
_____
_____
_____
_____
_____
_____
_____

Flavors

☐ Buttery ___%	☐ Lingering ___%	☐ Spicy ___%
☐ Grassy ___%	☐ Nutty ___%	☐ Sweet ___%
☐ Earthy ___%	☐ Pungent ___%	☐ Toasty ___%
☐ Herbal ___%	☐ Salty ___%	☐ _____ ___%
☐ Lactic ___%	☐ Sharp ___%	☐ _____ ___%

Rating

Appearance	☆☆☆☆☆	Comments: _____
Aroma	☆☆☆☆☆	_____
Taste	☆☆☆☆☆	_____

Overall Rating ☆☆☆☆☆   Buy Again: ◯ Yes   ◯ No

Name:

Origin: _____

Producer: _____

Age: _____ Date : _____

Price: _____

Milk

- ☐ Cow
- ☐ Sheep
- ☐ Goat
- ☐ Raw
- ☐ Other

_____
_____
_____

Texture

- ☐ Runny
- ☐ Soft
- ☐ Semi-soft
- ☐ Semi-firm
- ☐ Firm
- ☐ Hard

Notes

_____
_____
_____
_____
_____
_____
_____
_____

Flavors

☐ Buttery ___%	☐ Lingering ___%	☐ Spicy ___%
☐ Grassy ___%	☐ Nutty ___%	☐ Sweet ___%
☐ Earthy ___%	☐ Pungent ___%	☐ Toasty ___%
☐ Herbal ___%	☐ Salty ___%	☐ _____ ___%
☐ Lactic ___%	☐ Sharp ___%	☐ _____ ___%

Rating

Appearance ☆☆☆☆☆   Comments: _____

Aroma ☆☆☆☆☆   _____

Taste ☆☆☆☆☆   _____

Overall Rating ☆☆☆☆☆   Buy Again: ◯ Yes   ◯ No

Name:

Origin: _____

Producer: _____

Age: _____ Date : _____

Price: _____

Milk

☐ Cow
☐ Sheep
☐ Goat
☐ Raw
☐ Other
_____
_____
_____

Texture

☐ Runny
☐ Soft
☐ Semi-soft
☐ Semi-firm
☐ Firm
☐ Hard

Notes

_____
_____
_____
_____
_____
_____
_____
_____
_____

Flavors

☐ Buttery ___%	☐ Lingering ___%	☐ Spicy ___%
☐ Grassy ___%	☐ Nutty ___%	☐ Sweet ___%
☐ Earthy ___%	☐ Pungent ___%	☐ Toasty ___%
☐ Herbal ___%	☐ Salty ___%	☐ ___ ___%
☐ Lactic ___%	☐ Sharp ___%	☐ ___ ___%

Rating

Appearance ☆☆☆☆☆

Aroma ☆☆☆☆☆

Taste ☆☆☆☆☆

Comments: _____
_____
_____

Overall Rating ☆☆☆☆☆   Buy Again: ○ Yes   ○ No

Name:

Origin:_____

Producer:_____

Age:_____ Date :_____

Price:_____

Milk

- ☐ Cow
- ☐ Sheep
- ☐ Goat
- ☐ Raw
- ☐ Other
- _____
- _____
- _____

Texture

- ☐ Runny
- ☐ Soft
- ☐ Semi-soft
- ☐ Semi-firm
- ☐ Firm
- ☐ Hard

Notes

_____
_____
_____
_____
_____
_____
_____
_____

Flavors

☐ Buttery ___%	☐ Lingering ___%	☐ Spicy ___%
☐ Grassy ___%	☐ Nutty ___%	☐ Sweet ___%
☐ Earthy ___%	☐ Pungent ___%	☐ Toasty ___%
☐ Herbal ___%	☐ Salty ___%	☐ _____ ___%
☐ Lactic ___%	☐ Sharp ___%	☐ _____ ___%

Rating

Appearance ☆☆☆☆☆   Comments:_____

Aroma ☆☆☆☆☆   _____

Taste ☆☆☆☆☆   _____

Overall Rating ☆☆☆☆☆   Buy Again: ○ Yes   ○ No

Name:

Origin: _____

Producer: _____

Age: _____ Date : _____

Price: _____

Milk

- ☐ Cow
- ☐ Sheep
- ☐ Goat
- ☐ Raw
- ☐ Other

_____
_____
_____

Texture

- ☐ Runny
- ☐ Soft
- ☐ Semi-soft
- ☐ Semi-firm
- ☐ Firm
- ☐ Hard

Notes

_____
_____
_____
_____
_____
_____
_____
_____

Flavors

☐ Buttery ——%	☐ Lingering ——%	☐ Spicy ——%
☐ Grassy ——%	☐ Nutty ——%	☐ Sweet ——%
☐ Earthy ——%	☐ Pungent ——%	☐ Toasty ——%
☐ Herbal ——%	☐ Salty ——%	☐ —— ——%
☐ Lactic ——%	☐ Sharp ——%	☐ —— ——%

Rating

Appearance ☆☆☆☆☆   Comments: _____

Aroma ☆☆☆☆☆   _____

Taste ☆☆☆☆☆   _____

Overall Rating ☆☆☆☆☆   Buy Again: ◯ Yes   ◯ No

Notes

Notes

Notes

Notes

Notes